Spiral Tarot

A Story of the Cycles of Life

Spiral Tarot

A Story of the Cycles of Life

by Kay Steventon

Publishers
U.S. GAMES SYSTEMS, INC.
Stamford, CT 06902

For my Grandmother, Mary Anne O'Brien

Thank you to all my tutors, past, present, and future. Special thanks to Evelynne Joffe who introduced me to the mystical tradition of Kabbalistic teachings. Evelynne showed me how to tread the 32 paths. Thanks to Anne Shotter who guided me through the wisdom of the Tarot. Thanks also to Elaine Cox who typed these pages and to Mary Keane, my editor, adviser and old friend.

Copyright ©1998 by U.S. Games Systems, Inc.

Library of Congress Cataloging-in-Publication Data

Steventon, Kay
    Spiral Tarot: A Story of the Cycles of Life/Steventon.---1st ed.
      p. cm.
    Includes bibliographical references
    ISBN 1-57281-131-5 (pbk.)
    1. Tarot   I. Title
BF1879.T2 S747 1998
133.3'2424--ddc21   98-37323
                                         CIP

BK182

10 9 8 7 6 5 4 3 2

Publishers
U.S. GAMES SYSTEMS, INC.
Stamford, CT 06902 USA
Printed in Canada

Table of Contents

INTRODUCTION

The spiral is associated with regenerated life. This ancient symbol was and is used by diverse cultures on their monuments, in their art, and as part of religious rituals.

Like the symbol of the spiral, life is not a straight road; it twists and turns through a forest of experiences. Each phase begins, moves to a climax and comes to conclusion only to move into a new experience as the process begins again. We spiral in and out of cycles. Like the seasons, we are renewed in spring, ripened in summer, and gather our harvest in autumn. In winter, what is no longer useful is left to decay, nourishing the soil for new life when spring returns.

This continuum of life from a Kabbalistic viewpoint is described as the spark of life originating in Kether at the top of the Tree of Life and spiraling down to take form in Malkuth before ascending the Tree again as matter evolves into spirit.

If we look beyond ourselves to the workings of the Cosmos, the spiral appears again. In our galaxy, the planets revolve around the sun in a spiral pattern. Our earth makes this journey every year, but never repeats precisely the path of the year before. In astrology, as the planets move around and around a person's birthchart, the contacts of the transiting planets with natal planets are significant. At these times, the individual has the opportunity to make changes, begin or end a cycle, and hopefully grow towards personal wisdom.

The journey the Fool makes through the tarot is that same spiraling process. He begins the journey, lives the experience, and comes to the end of that phase only to start afresh. He repeats the process, but like all cycles in nature, the new phase is different from the last.

There has been much discussion about the origins of the tarot. Whatever their origins, the fact that the tarot cards still mystify and fascinate many followers reinforces my belief that the twenty-two Major Arcana are universal archetypes, reflecting the sum of our journey through life. They symbolize all the characters and stages that influence our development as human beings. These archetypes are just as relevant today as they were centuries ago.

As a child, I gained my first education into the mysteries of the tarot from my grandmother, who used to "read" the playing cards. I took this procedure for granted and had no idea I would develop a deep involvement with the cards and their complex meanings much later in my life. My grandmother promised she would try to reach me "one way or another" after her death. I have the feeling she has been behind me all through this process, guiding my thoughts. Thus I chose the late 1800s as the period to depict the Minor Arcana cards in honor of her birthday.

The following pages attempt to describe our complete life cycle from birth to old age, and are not meant to be definitive. They are just another way of approaching and endeavoring to understand the journey through the tarot. The tarot is multi-layered; we can view it at a purely spiritual level or consider only the mundane realities of a person's life.

For each of the twenty-two Major Arcana cards, I have chosen what I regard as an appropriate myth to describe the message of the archetype. I centered my attention on a mixture of Middle Eastern, Arthurian, and Mediterranean myths because I am familiar with them. However, I believe myths from any culture would be just as appropriate, considering the universality of the cards. The major cards in the *Spiral Tarot* deck incorporate brief facets of related disciplines the reader may already have knowledge of. I have included rudimentary comments on the Kabbalah and Astrology that I believe correspond to and enhance the tarot. For further information on these subjects, refer to Suggested Readings at the back of this book.

My renewed involvement in the tarot began some years ago. At the time I thought the knowledge would simply extend my already dedicated interest in astrology and mythology. It was not until I became involved with a group of ardent esoteric students that I realized the profundity of the twenty-two Major Arcana. Encouraged by my colleagues, I became enthusiastic about using my artistic training to create my own tarot deck. Soon I found myself recreating my own journey through life, with all of its pain, loss, and joy.

Everyone's journey is the same, and yet at the same time quite different. We all begin life innocent, willing to learn and take part in this wonderworld. We do not know the pitfalls that life has to offer; nor do we know that inevitably we stand alone, separate and mortal. We are the innocent Fool.

It seems to me the ultimate message of the tarot is that we need to blend and unite every aspect of our personality, the good and the bad. We must not deny those parts of ourselves we are not so keen on, but accept who we are. The tarot images, like us, have positive and negative sides to their messages; we learn from them what is inherent in us. The Fool's journey occurs many times in one lifetime. We start the cycle, live through it, and reach the ultimate end, like the winding and unwinding of the spiral.

GETTING TO KNOW YOUR CARDS

When we begin to learn the meaning of the cards, seventy-eight images seem daunting. However, with patience and practice they will become familiar friends.

Starting with the Major Arcana cards, it is a good idea to study or meditate on each one separately. The main goal is to develop the intuitive process by asking yourself questions: How do you respond to each card? What symbols stand out for you? How does the card make you feel? After a time the cards will "speak" to you. When you start practicing readings for yourself, family and friends, getting to know the different combinations of cards becomes more complicated. It is necessary at this stage to refer to the book constantly until you become more confident.

The cards should be treated with respect, but in my opinion it is not necessary to wrap them in silk or have a special wooden box in which to place them. It is not the cards, but the messages behind the images that are important.

THE JOURNEY

The first character we meet in the play of life is the Magician. He stays with us all our lives. From the moment of birth we use the Magician's skills; we learn to communicate our bodily needs to our mother or caretaker with screaming cries and flailing arms and legs. Then we learn language by which we are able to communicate with fellow humans and to explore the wonders of the world through books and schooling.

We continue to learn for the rest of our lives, sometimes having to repeat the same mistakes, trying to get it right. The Magician keeps us on our toes. We know the Magician's good points, but we always have to watch out for his negative aspect, the Trickster. He usually appears when our ego becomes inflated and we think we know all the answers.

Although she is next to appear in the tarot, in our very early years we cannot access the wisdom of the High Priestess. We are taught in schools and religious institutions about a father God who is all powerful; both fearsome and benevolent. Western culture generally ignores God's female counterpart. Much later in life when we contact the High Priestess, it suddenly dawns on us that she lives within and has been there all along, just waiting to be recognized. We see her darkness and her light when we meet her. She is the cold, calculating feminine figure who devours her creations, and the intuitive feminine figure who holds the keys to wisdom and understanding.

The Magician and the High Priestess are the prime motivators who bring about our conception, after which we meet the Empress. She is the mother who held you to her warm breast, nourishing you with her milk and love. She is our first love. At the beginning of life, she is our world. For a man, her influence will determine how he relates to women later in life. For women, mother is a role model who teaches us how to be women. The positive Empress gives unconditional love; she is fertile and creative. The negative Empress will try to hang on to us. She does not allow growth, denies life and squashes our creativity.

Our father is our second love. When we see beyond our mother's breast, Father is there, the Emperor. In his positive aspect he provides for, guides and protects us from harm. We can rely on him; he is stable and dependable and teaches us how to develop our own authority. He becomes his daughter's hero and will influence her choice in men later. Dad is his son's role model; the son will want to emulate the father. The negative Emperor is the domineering, harsh, brutal father, who crushes the spirit. He can also present as the distant father who never supports you, or is never there when you need him. We carry the influence of the Emperor and the Empress with us for the rest of our lives, even into our marriage bed.

Affected by these influences, we now go out into the world for the first time on our own, ready or not. We meet the Hierophant. With the Magician in the back wings, we take out our pencils and paper. Suddenly the whole world opens up, with all its rules, regulations, and wonders. We learn we cannot do just what we want; we must conform to other children in the class. That is just the beginning. When we leave school we find more rules and regulations in the work place, law, and government. With all this, we still have to speak our own truth in a world of conformity.

When the positive aspect of the Hierophant comes into being, we begin to question our traditional background. We know that all we have been told is not necessarily true. We are now able to form our own opinions and beliefs, while still accepting society. The negative aspect of the Hierophant expresses itself when there is such rigid conformity to convention that we have no opinions, and we are too timid to step out of the mold.

In our next phase, we come under the influence of the Lovers. We fall in love, discover our sexuality and have to become responsible for our passions. We must try to discriminate between the many partner possibilities that present themselves. Choosing the right partner is not an easy task; we may suffer a broken heart along the way, or live through many relationship scenarios. The influence of parents, siblings and others all contribute to our choices, and these choices have a significant effect on the direction of our lives, which is where the next card becomes important.

As we deal with the effects of the Lovers, we meet the Chariot and start to wonder where our lives are heading. Our youth was yesterday; where has time gone? We need to get out into the world and make our mark. We now have the impetus to become someone, and the determination and willpower to succeed. Now mature, we probably have family responsibilities. There is no longer room for the romantic ideals of youth; we have to be more single-minded and purposeful.

The mid-life crisis comes at this stage. There is something stirring deep inside us; we feel restless and have to fight impulses to drop everything and run. But we do not: not yet, for we have entered the phase represented by Strength.

At this point, we might have reached the top of our particular establishment tree. We may be balanced between a healthy sense of pride in our achievements and arrogance peppered with ambition. We have learned the techniques of dealing with people in the business world or other arenas, and we have found various ways of keeping our feelings and yearnings in check. An internal struggle begins. The wild beast is struggling to emerge; this beast is lust. Lust in any form is dangerous, but the lust for power, for control of others, is perhaps the worst. These feelings of restlessness at the time of the mid-life crisis need a great deal of self-examination and self-control. Life is beckoning. The question arises: what have we missed? Lust is prodding us; we think perhaps a young or new lover will rejuvenate us.

As these thoughts and feelings are milling about in our heads, the smart ones among us consult the Hermit. We need to go deep inside ourselves for the answers. No one else can make the decisions for us now. We can no longer blame our parents, or the terrible upbringing we had; the answers lie deep within our hearts. We may need to withdraw from the busy world to a place of serenity where we can be with our thoughts. This is a period of self-examination. What do I really want from life? Have I lived life with integrity until now? Do I have regrets I cannot reconcile? We need to know where we stand, for the Wheel of Fortune is turning.

Who is ready for the change the Wheel of Fortune brings? Some of us welcome the change, for life has become too pre-dictable. We are prepared to throw away everything we have gained so far. Others may try to hang on to what they have in a desperate attempt to keep equilibrium in their lives. It makes no difference. Events will occur over which we seem to have little control, which change our lives forever. The Wheel of Fortune, as the name implies, can bring good or bad fortune. It depends to some extent on the decisions one has made in life and one's ability to accept consequences. It also depends on whether we have acted on the opportunities life has offered.

After we have made changes in our lives, willingly or not, it is payback time when Justice appears. If we have taken too much from life, Justice will expect us to contribute. There is the possibility that Justice could represent the divorce court after the effect of the Wheel of Fortune. We are certainly old enough and have had enough experience to know whether we are fair. Do we take much more than we give back in our relationships, business dealings or our community? Justice has the habit of exacting payment, one way or another. We may look back and wish we had taken the advice of the Hermit, or had dealt with the energy of the Wheel in a different way.

The major lesson Justice offers is to accept the judgment as a result of decisions we make; we cannot get it right every time. This is the first step towards balancing the different parts of ourselves, the good and the bad. The Wheel of Fortune marks the middle of our journey. Some of us stay on the treadmill forever; some retreat, with fear as the prime culprit. It's easy to understand those of us who stay where we are because the path is easier and far more comfortable. However, after Justice and acceptance of our karmic debt, we can meet the Hanged Man.

Our lives have been turned upside-down. We just hang, not knowing what will happen next. This stage brings with it the first glimmering of something greater than the self. We must trust that life will not let us down; that we will not hang there forever. We are being initiated into viewing life with a far different perspective than we have had before. This initiation requires some form of self-sacrifice and usually means a surrender of our ego-consciousness. We become more aware that we are a part of a whole.

This is the first step toward individuation and requires a great deal of patience and faith that we will be all right. This is the turning point. If we lack faith in ourselves and life, we are in danger of becoming victims. Then we will lose our way, unable to see any future in this vale of tears. We might try to survive by throwing ourselves into all kinds of activities; anything that will avoid the pain of having to deal with hurtful issues. If we learn to sit with it, feel it, give in and let go, something shifts.

If we surrender our ego, Death sweeps in and every false notion we held as truth falls away. We feel stripped bare; some of us are dragged into the underworld, a dark place of depression and despair. It is a great trial for us to overcome the loss of self in darkness. However, we somehow crawl back renewed, having shed the baggage of the past. We have walked through the dark recesses of the soul during our time in the Underworld and have reached an understanding of who we are, a greater knowledge of the Self.

Thankfully, at this point Temperance steps in to renew the balance in our lives. This time balance is not about weighing and measuring past actions and deeds. Temperance is about inner balance, about hope after despair, and enlightenment after ignorance. We feel a sense of inner peace; our lives have become more fulfilling and our function in the outer world is productive. At this stage some may decide to enjoy a continuing state of harmony. We feel good after the experiences we have survived. For others, however, the quest is not yet over. The Hanged Man has shown us the gateway to self-knowledge; standing at the entrance, we confront the Devil.

If we are to undertake the final part of our journey of integration, we have to dig further into the recesses of the unconscious to face our Shadow. (Readers who want to understand more about the Shadow should read Jung on the topic.) Again, we are faced with a choice. If we choose to confront our Shadow, there is no turning back and no guarantee of success. For this reason, some of us choose not to risk this step; this is an important and viable choice.

Those of us who feel we have no choice but to keep going, must have the maturity to grapple with what the Devil is asking of us and what is meant by this confrontation, or we will surely fail. The Devil tempts us; he seduces us to reveal our true nature. Thus we see, mirrored in his face, our Shadow. All our projections, the faults we see in others, are really our own.

Unconscious fears are our worst enemy and the Devil's friend. We cannot go further on the journey until we deal with those fears. We are being challenged to take responsibility for who we are, warts and all. The choice lies in owning our projections and fears and the destruction that arises from them for not doing so. If, having chosen this path, we retreat at this critical point, our Shadow, triumphant, becomes obsessive in the material world. All the things that keep us blind to choice, like addictions, power, wealth and lust will rule us. However, if we know and accept who we are, we can enjoy the material world without being possessed by it.

Now appears a very frightening image: the Tower. It is for those of us who, having reached a certain level of enlightenment, imagine that we know it all. We think of ourselves as evolved souls. We do not need to go any further, for what more is there to know? Now that we have dared to face our Shadow, we think we can afford to sit back and allow a feeling of accomplishment to sweep over us and elevate us to a position of false pride. What happened to that ego we surrendered way back with the Hanged Man? The ego is part of our psyche; there is a big difference between a healthy ego and an inflated one.

If we think we have won status with the Gods, we are soon put back in our place. When the Tower appears, we are likely to be thrown down as a reminder of our humanity. In the eyes of the gods, not one of us is necessarily more blessed than the other. After the enlightenment of the lightning flash, we learn the lesson of humility. If our foundations are solid, the Tower energy will simply give us a necessary shake-up and will leave the way open to continue our journey.

After we have been knocked off our ivory tower, we are very pleased to see the light of the Star. We need her renewed faith and promise that life has still got a lot to offer; we are not finished yet. We feel good, we still feel very connected to life even after the trials we have experienced. The Star is the essence of the human spirit. This spirit will not be daunted while the light of the Star shines brightly. There is a greater feeling of balance than ever before. There is no longer any need for pretense, for we accept and love ourselves in a way neither humble nor arrogant, but as we are.

We are led now by the Moon to the world of the unconscious, where all memories from the beginning of life and beyond reside. At last we can tap into the energies of the High Priestess. It is only now that her wisdom and knowledge begin to make sense. We go back to our primal roots when we encounter the Moon, back to birth and before. In a way we see the whole journey displayed before us: the monsters of childhood, the emotional depth we thought we had outgrown. We re-experience our mothers, the parenting we had and all its implications. For women, this time can be symbolic of menopause, as the Empress is of our fertile years; for us, the Moon suggests getting in touch with the wise old woman within. For men, their inner feminine guide can become powerful. In either case, the Moon's gift is heightened intuition and wisdom.

After visiting the unconscious world and confronting what is left of our personal monsters, we find ourselves in the full light of day and consciousness. We embrace the light and warmth of the Sun; we feel the load of life lifting off our shoulders. Like children, we feel free. We could stay in that place; indeed, some of us do, by slipping into dementia and becoming the child again.

For the rest of us, a renewal of energy occurs when Judgment blows his trumpet. Again we seem to be faced with a choice. In this phase, there may not be any real choice; perhaps the call to rebirth is predestined.

Finally, I do not know if anyone, other than the archetypal Fool, directly experiences the energy of the World card. It is the resolution that occurs before rebirth and the beginning of the Fool's journey and ours once more. This cycle, of course, can occur many times during our lives on the material plane. Possibly, those of us who have a creative and spiritual physical death might at that point consciously experience the energy of this card. The World is perfection, the total integration of all things. As to the end, we shall just have to wait and see.

THE MAJOR ARCANA

0 THE FOOL

Key words: Faith. Trust in life. Optimism. New beginnings.

Myth

In the card of the Fool we meet young Perceval. He wears the simple homespun garment his mother has made for him. Around his waist he wears a belt of laurel leaves, reminding us of the victories won in life; attached to the belt is a small bag containing courage, optimism, loyalty, and fearlessness. This bag also contains the memory of many lifetimes and many journeys that lie just below the surface of consciousness. The object of his quest is to begin the Spiral Journey once more with renewed confidence and faith.

Perceval was an ordinary youth who had grown up in a forest, reared by his widowed mother. He had no knowledge of worldly ways, so when a group of knights rode into the forest, he was so overwhelmed by their splendid appearance he vowed to become a knight. Perceval's mother wept to see her son go. However, she gave him her blessing and the warning not to ask too many questions.

On his journey, after some adventures, Perceval found King Arthur's court. Soon after entering the castle, Perceval asked to be knighted. The courtly knights and ladies all laughed at the simple country boy dressed in homespun. Arthur told Perceval he had to learn to become a knight.

Perceval learned knightly skills from an old nobleman named Gournamond, who told him to go out into the world and find the Fisher King's castle where the Grail was kept. Gournamond also told Perceval to ask the question, "Whom does the Grail serve?"

When Perceval found the Grail castle, the Fisher King was lying on a litter in great pain. He had been wounded in the groin. The people were there enjoying a banquet. Soon a maiden entered the hall carrying the Grail and each guest made a wish which the Grail granted. The king, however, could not join the others because of his wound.

Perceval remembered his instructions to ask, "Whom does the Grail serve?" He also remembered his mother telling him not to ask questions. Perceval remained silent and the Grail, king and castle disappeared.

Perceval would not give up his search for the Grail and its suffering king. He spent many years wandering the barren land where nothing would grow. People and animals were dying, a reflection of their ailing king. After many battles and contests Perceval met a forest hermit who, after scolding him for not asking the question in the first place, guided him to the Grail castle.

Perceval found exactly the same scene; the banquet, the maiden, the Grail and the Fisher King still lying in pain.

Perceval asked the question, "Whom does the Grail serve?" Magically, the king and the land were restored to health and vigor. The Grail serves the king.

The Grail myths sprang from sixth century Celtic regions and developed through the middle ages to the present day.

The legendary King Arthur is assumed to have reigned in England when Christianity was taking over from the ancient pagan religion. The Arthurian myths were developed from earlier Celtic stories. There are references to objects that historians regard as precursors to the Grail, for example, the god Bran's cauldron of rebirth, the platter that was always laden with food. Sometimes the early Grail was a bowl, a cup or even a stone.

As people became more Christianized, the Grail was said to be the chalice used by Christ at the last supper. It was believed the same chalice received his blood at the crucifixion.

The Fisher King is wounded in the groin/genitals; he cannot function as a man. He is as barren as the land he rules, for the king has lost contact with the feminine (the Grail). Here is a split between spirit and nature, the god and the goddess. It is through the pure of heart, the simple, innocent fool, Perceval, that the king is healed and the restoration of the waste land is accomplished.

The Grail becomes that which is attained and realized by people who have lived their own lives. The Grail represents the fulfillment of the highest spiritual potentialities of the human consciousness.[1]

In the card, Perceval looks in wonderment and awe at the grail image, the symbol of his quest in life. An angel is there to protect and watch over him. Perceval is also accompanied by a black cat, a feminine image close to nature. The masculine needs a feminine guide if the Grail is to be found; the cat instinctively senses danger, whereas the Fool is fearless. Eagles, symbols of kingly spirit, soar over an abyss which is very deep and dark.

The card of the Fool is associated with the planet Uranus, symbol of freedom and the quest for humankind's highest ideals. It is also an abstract airy planet; pure spirit is the converse of earth and nature. Uranus symbolizes abstract thought. At this stage, the Fool is an abstraction. He needs to make the journey to become real and grounded. The moment he commences the journey, he enters the realm of consciousness. The Fool is pure masculine energy, so when he sees the Grail, he is driven on by some unconscious force to attain whatever it is the Grail offers. He knows instinctively the Grail symbol is the means to make him whole.

On the Kabbalistic Tree of Life, the Fool walks the eleventh path between Kether, limitless light and Chokmah, celestial father. The Fool signifies innocence of the spirit coming forth into manifestation. The eleventh path is the path of complete simplicity; here total inexperience moves with the wisdom of the Divine informing it. Just so, the Fool is like the breath of life, a vibrant emptiness waiting to be filled. The corresponding Hebrew letter is Aleph, which means Ox. Aleph is a channel by which the infinite spiritual is brought to the infinite physical. The Aleph is said to contain the essence of all other letters.

Divinatory Meaning

The card of the Fool signifies a time to follow our own intuitive, instinctive natures. With this card, we should step into life fearlessly and without prejudice; we should never waver from the quest. The Fool succeeds through his unfaltering journey. He is true to himself, trusting his judgment and having faith in what lies beyond the abyss.

I THE MAGICIAN

**Key words: Magic. Communication. Creative intellect.
Power of thought. Pure masculine energy.**

Myth

Hermes the Magician, as messenger of the gods, has direct
access to the Divine. He is the principal masculine life force who
makes manifest divine power. By way of the intellect we can
access that power in a modified form. Hermes represents the
countless possibilities of the universe available to humankind.
He is the thinking principle, the thought before consciousness,
the spark or flash of insight that seemingly comes from nowhere.

Hermes was the son of Zeus, the supreme Greek god, and
Maia, "Grandmother of Magic." When Hermes was only one

day old, he displayed his cleverness by leaving his cradle and stealing Apollo's cattle, as well as devising a way to conceal the theft. Apollo used his power of divination to discover the thief. Hermes denied all knowledge of the deed, so Apollo took Hermes to Zeus. Father Zeus was amused and thought Hermes an ingenious, eloquent, and persuasive godling. Still, he ordered Hermes to return the cattle. Hermes then asked his father to make him the heavenly herald and keeper of all divine property. He promised to never tell lies, but could not promise to always tell the truth.

To appease Apollo, Hermes again used his cleverness to fashion the first musical instrument, the lyre, out of a tortoise shell (early animal symbol of the universe). This he swapped for Apollo's cattle. He then made a pipe out of reeds and played a wonderful tune. Apollo immediately bartered his golden staff, the caduceus, for the pipe.

The Triple Muse (mountain goddesses) taught Hermes divination by means of dancing pebbles on water. Hermes was the god of the alphabet, travelers, commerce, magic, and tricksters and was responsible for inventing fire. Hades (god of the Underworld) also engaged Hermes to become the Psychopomp, he who guides souls to the underworld after death.

Hermes is identified with the Egyptian god of intelligence, Thoth, and the Germanic god Wotan in his aspect of conductor of souls.

In the card of the Magician, Hermes holds the caduceus aloft, thus making divine energy manifest. This is represented by a fertile tree bearing fruit. On the caduceus are two intertwined serpents, ancient symbols of healing and renewal. The dual serpents also indicate Hermes's function as lord of death and re-birth. In another myth, Hermes was responsible for saving the infant Dionysus from death so that he could be reborn from father Zeus's thigh. Hermes was the patron of alchemy, as his caduceus had the magical power to turn objects into gold.

On Hermes's cape are the four symbols of the Minor Arcana. The Cup (or Grail) is the feminine water element, representing the emotions, feelings, creativity, and love. The Sword is the masculine air element, representing the intellect, logic, reason, and questioning powers. The Wand is the masculine fire element, representing intuition, vision, and action. The Pentacle is the feminine earth element, representing growth, structure, practical matters, and life.

Hermes has all the elements at his disposal, indicated by the sunlit sky and, by contrast, the shifting clouds. He wears winged sandals that can take him anywhere, anytime. He is shown here with one foot in the inner world, the unknown unconscious realm, and the other foot in the world of the manifest. Thus he bridges both worlds.

Hermes/Mercury rules the astrological sign Gemini, the twins. Gemini symbolizes the two faces of the god as evidenced by the duality of his character. He is god of commerce, lawful and unlawful, trickster and wizard, teacher and wise man. The planet Mercury is the airy communicator. In the solar system, Mercury is never more than twenty-eight degrees away from the Sun, symbolic of being close to the source. Mercury signifies the power of union. Without communication and movement, union becomes impossible. It is the quest of humankind to create wholeness and unity. With communication, either oral or written, we may learn all things, past, present, and future. Mercury represents the thought that precedes action. Thought is abstract, we cannot physically hold it; it flits into our minds and just as easily slips away. This is like the god, who with winged feet is elusive: Now you see him, now you don't. He is both the Trickster and the treasure trove of Knowledge.

On the Kabbalistic Tree of Life the Magician walks the twelfth path from Kether the crown, source and great organizer, to Binah the supernal mother, meaning understanding. The twelfth path is the path of realization of personal abilities and knowledge of personal powers. It is where the vision of the true plan and how it can be made manifest becomes clear. The letter is Beth, meaning house or temple, the dwelling place of the spirit descending into manifestation.

Divinatory Meaning

When the Magician appears in a spread, something magical or miraculous is about to happen. The skills of the universe are there for you. Important communication may manifest in the form of letters, meetings, or telecommunications. You may have a clear-sighted vision for some future project, or a project already started may become more easily achievable. You may now know what is needed to succeed and be able to gauge the right time to proceed with any plans. You have the power to make things happen. Any creative idea could become reality. Make sure the plan is reasonable. At this stage ideas are in their infancy; use the skills of the Magician to think things through in a logical fashion, or the trickster might appear.

II THE HIGH PRIESTESS
**Key words: Intuition. Independence. Insight. Patience.
Self-sufficiency. Reflection.**

Myth

According to the Gnostic sect that appeared around the first century AD, Jesus was conceived in the mind of the Holy Spirit, who in the Hebrew language was a female. The male Holy Ghost was created by the Romans through direct translation of the name. It was also the case that early Christians mistrusted female deities. The Gnostics, whose language was Greek, identified the Holy Spirit with Sophia, wisdom, who, like the High Priestess, was also female.[2]

In *Symbols of Transformation*, Jung states that the ancients saw woman as either Eve (impulsive), Helen (emotional), Sophia (intelligence) or Mary (moral). The Goddess in her wholeness has been fragmented. Her many attributes have been distributed to many deities. It is important to look beyond the many Goddesses' attributes and to realize that they are all part of a whole. Sophia is present in all her aspects; that is why in the next card, she flies above the head of the Empress in the form of a dove, for the bird both honors Aphrodite/Venus by signifying sexual passion and symbolizes the soul returning to the Goddess at death.

Sophia is associated with the Egyptian Goddess Isis/Hathor and, in a much later time, the Christian Virgin Mary, Mother of God.[3]

The many symbols on the High Priestess card are to acknowledge some of the varied goddesses who are aspects of Sophia. The columns on either side of the card are Egyptian in character, in deference to Isis/Hathor. The Greek Sphinx forming part of the throne is the goddess Urania in her light and dark aspects. She has dominion over air and earth and delegates sovereignty to her royal son, the King.[4] Palm fronds adorn the veil behind the High Priestess, symbols for Innana/Ishtar. The pomegranates are sacred to Persephone. Cerberus, the three-headed wolf, belongs to Hecate, goddess of the dark and unknown. The wolf guards the gates of the underworld (the unconscious), where only the brave may enter. A fire burns in the Sibyl's tripod; the High Priestess sees the Fool's past, present, and future unfolding in the dancing flames and swirling smoke.

The High Priestess as Sophia holds the key to universal knowledge as God's equal: a knowledge of the structure of the world and the operation of the elements; the beginning and the end of epochs and their middle course; the alternative solstices and the changing seasons; the cycles of the years and constellations. "I learned it all, hidden or manifest, for I was taught by Her whose skill made all things, Wisdom (Sophia)."[5]

Sophia remains aloof and mysterious, far removed from humankind. We cannot comprehend the breadth or depth of her wise knowledge. As God's counterpart, we cannot know her just as we cannot know God in His magnificence. In the card of the High Priestess, Sophia sits despondently. She does not look at us because we have failed to acknowledge her. The Tora lies casually in her lap; all the secrets of the universe are contained in this scroll. The knowledge is available to us, for the High Priestess does not attempt to hide or disguise this precious document.

However, there is a secret dark side to the High Priestess that is not accessible to us. In this aspect she is the goddess Persephone, Queen of the Underworld, whose secrets are kept hidden in the darkness. Her knowledge expresses itself in the form of knowing a right decision has been made, or sensing impending danger. She is the intuitive process that we must learn to trust.

The High Priestess card is associated with the Moon, the prime feminine principle, in its dark unknown aspect. The astrological moon rules memory, unconscious yearnings and the past.

The dark moon is felt by the Fool during times of isolation and when he experiences the dark night of the soul. The High Priestess is the Grail Maiden, that is, the Keeper of the Grail. The Fool can access its healing powers when the right question is asked. The High Priestess will make available to the Fool some of her wise counsel during times of aloneness, or when he is feeling lost and experiencing deep feelings he cannot explain.

The High Priestess walks the thirteenth path on the Kabbalistic Tree of Life. She bridges the dark abyss between Kether the crown, God the father, and Tiphareth, beauty, the son of God. The High Priestess unites with the masculine as Sophia, the Holy Spirit.

The Hebrew letter is Gimel, meaning camel. The camel can sustain itself through the desert abyss; the High Priestess is associated with the element water. She can lead us through the desert. We will not die of thirst if we dare to cross the abyss with free will and no pretenses.

Divinatory Meaning

In a reading, the High Priestess signifies experiencing deep feelings. There may be a yearning to deepen our intuitive powers. It could be a time to act independently, using our own resourcefulness to gain insight to a personal dilemma. We have the opportunity to become more self-sufficient. This is not the time to rush into things. When the High Priestess appears, she is telling us to be patient, to be still and listen to our inner voice for the answers. The High Priestess can bestow great insight into all matters. She can unravel mysteries if we are prepared to reflect and trust ourselves.

When the High Priestess appears as a real person, she could be the older woman who offers good advice. She may be the woman who lives alone, or she may be the mother who turns her back on you. She could also be the intuitive mystery woman you are drawn to. You could experience a time of loneliness or isolation. In that case, use the time constructively, listen to dreams and meditate. The High Priestess can help you gain greater insight into the underlying mystery of a problem. Don't be afraid to be alone.

III THE EMPRESS

**Key words: Creativity. Productivity. Compassion.
Unconditional Love. Sensuality.
Smothering love. Jealousy. Possessiveness.**

Myth

Mother-Goddess cults flourished throughout Europe
and the Near East during ancient history. The mythology
behind many of the Greek/Roman goddesses reaches back
to matrilineal times when the goddess was accorded a great
deal of power and reverence.

In the earliest period of human history people were nomadic;
hunting and gathering were their primary means of survival.
These early people eventually invented agriculture, which en-
abled them to settle in one place. This was a major change in

their relationship with the earth, which was reflected in the nature of their spiritual beliefs.

The bountiful land was seen as the goddess; the hills and valleys were the contours of her body, the rivers her life-giving blood. The goddess cults were associated with the changing seasons and the natural rhythms of life. Women were honored because their monthly cycle and their ability to be fruitful mirrored the goddess. As the seasons changed, winter was understood as the mother taking back into her womb the decay of the previous season to nurture the soil for the coming cycle. Then the birth of new growth in spring led to the harvest in summer. The Mother Goddess loved her children; even after death, she regenerated life.

The garden of the Empress is the original Garden of Eden before the fall, where growth flourishes, trees bear fruit, and the grain is plentiful. Life in ancient Crete, which was a matrilineal society, was seen as such a paradise. The eighth century Greek poet, Hesiod, describing Crete, said: "The earth poured forth its fruits unbidden in boundless plenty. In peaceful ease they kept their lands with good abundance, rich in flocks."

In this Cretan paradise, just as in Eden, the snake played a central role; but the meaning attributed to the creature in each case could not have been more different. Through their snake goddess, the Cretans revered the snake for its healing and regenerative powers and associated it with the Earth Mother's cyclic process. However, in later biblical texts the snake became synonymous with evil, the Earth Mother lost her significance, and Eve and the snake were held responsible for the expulsion from Paradise.

In classical Greece, the Earth Mother was known as Demeter, goddess of the grain. She was responsible for the fecundity of the land. By this time, the attributes of the Great Goddess were distributed among many deities.

Demeter had a daughter, Persephone. The god Hades abducted Persephone and took her to his realm, the Underworld, where he made her his queen. These two goddesses, Demeter and Persephone, show the light and dark aspects of the Empress. On one hand, the Empress as Demeter symbolizes consciousness: she lives in the upper world and is loving, giving, and fertile. On the other hand, Persephone, queen of the Underworld, symbolizes the unconscious dark nature of the Empress. In this state, she is unreceptive, withholding her love and creativity.

The Empress card is associated with the planet Venus/Aphrodite. Venus rules both the astrological signs Libra and Taurus. The sign Libra describes the Empress's needs for relationship and love, her eye for beauty and harmonious surroundings. The sign Taurus connects her to the earth and her fertile sensual nature. Taurus the Bull was associated with the early Mother Goddess cults. In many mythologies the bull was the consort of the goddess, and rituals were performed yearly to ensure the fertility of the land. In many cultures, the bull was known as the corn spirit and was usually slaughtered at the harvest of the crops.

In the card the Empress wears a gown of red and green, the colors of fertility. Red roses adorn her gown and cape. The rose is sacred to Venus in its voluptuous perfume, texture, and form. In her hand, the Empress holds a spiral, indicating she holds the secrets of the seasons and of the life/death process (the thread of life). Her foot rests on a crescent moon, her connection with the feminine principle. Above her head flies a white dove, symbolic of God's female soul. Her scepter terminates in a combined Venus/Sun symbol, showing the Empress's desire for union with the masculine principle. The waterfall behind the throne is symbolic of the Waters of Life and the Empress's connection with the unconscious realm of the High Priestess and the Moon. The Empress's garden is full of poppies, lilies, ripe wheat, apples, and pomegranates. Her garden is indeed flourishing; in fact it might revert to jungle if the Emperor does not come along soon to do a little pruning.

The bright glowing disk behind the Empress is symbolic of the Evening Star, the Goddess of Love. The "glad eyed Ishtar of desire, the Goddess of sighing... whose song is sweeter than sprouts and herbs, superior even to pure cream."[6] As the morning star, the Goddess arrayed herself in armor ready to do battle. The Empress has a negative aspect. Her battledress can take the form of possessiveness, jealousy and 'smother' love.

The positive aspect of the Empress archetype represents boundless love. Here is the sensual lover who encourages relationship. The Empress is the mother who loves unconditionally and forgives her children when they transgress. Her creative potential and productivity know no boundaries.

The negative Empress manipulates her lovers and her offspring; she can be the complaining martyr mother or the possessive dragon suggested by the traditional stereotype of the mother-in-law. Sometimes she is simply the mother who does not respond to your needs.

The Emperor is the Empress's consort and opposite. He needs her love and compassion and she needs his ability to discern, to have self-discipline and control. He needs her generous heart; in return she needs his restraint.

On the Kabbalistic Tree of Life, the Empress walks the fourteenth path, between Chokmah, wisdom, the supernal father, and Binah, understanding, the supernal mother. The path of the Empress joins the two pillars representing the masculine and feminine forces. The letter is Daleth, meaning door: the door of knowledge, transition and illumination.

Divinatory Meaning

When the Empress appears in a spread, she may indicate a fruitful period in our lives. Our creative urge to be productive may become pressing. Mother, lover, wife issues could come into focus. The creative Empress, in her positive aspect teaches us to love but not to smother. The creative artist must learn to let go of his or her creations; the loving mother must ultimately let go of her children.

IV THE EMPEROR

**Key words: Structure. Authority. Leadership. Father.
Responsibility. Control. Arrogance. Ruthlessness.**

Myth

The legendary King Arthur was born to Igraine around the year
500 AD. Although Igraine was the wife of Duke Gorlois, the
father of Igraine's child was Uther, Pendragon of Britain. Some
authorities say Arthur was born at the fortress castle Tintagel.

Myth has it that Merlin the magician manipulated the union
of Arthur's parents to keep the royal line of kings alive. Merlin
raised Arthur, educating him in the laws of nature, magic, and
bardic traditions.

When Arthur was ready for the throne, the country was going
through a dark period. The Roman invaders, after many years,

retreated to Rome taking with them the protection of their armies. Britain was constantly harassed by the invaders from the north, while at the same time internal war was waged between the Romanized Christians and those who were fighting to keep the old pagan religion alive.

Arthur held the balance between old and new. The ancient traditions, language, customs, and reverence for the goddess of the land stood against the progressive new ways of a Roman legacy which included Christianity and exclusion of the goddess.

The last of the Celtic kings, Arthur led many battles, culminating in the battle at Badon, after which peace reigned for the next twenty years. King Arthur met his death during the battle at Camlan, when he and his nephew (some say his son) were both mortally wounded. Arthur was taken by sea to the magical isle of apples, Avalon, where he died. It is said that Arthur lies asleep waiting to rise again when his country needs him.

In the card of the Emperor, Arthur sits on his throne. He is dressed for battle. The throne is solid, bearing a Roman influence in its columns. The double-headed eagle behind him reminds us of his supreme dominion and divine majesty over the material universe. The eagle symbolizes Zeus the Father and is associated with power and authority. The Emperor's head is encased in chain mail so his head is divorced from his body. This reminds us we cannot live by intellect alone.

The Emperor represents the rational mind, without which we would not be able to make decisions or function in the modern world. The Emperor gives us stability, order, and self-discipline. He is as solid as his throne and the rocks on which it is built. The dilemma is, nothing can grow in this rocky place. Arthur has lost connection with the feminine. The black and white checker-board under his feet represents the Celtic goddess of the land. In ancient times the king was consort to this goddess. When the king ruled in harmony with his realm, the land flourished. When the king ailed, so did the land. In a negative sense, too much Emperor without a little goddess energy leads to arrogance and narrow thinking. There needs to be a balance between intellect, the conscious mind, and feeling. The union of the king and the land is symbolic of the union of the masculine and feminine within us.

The Grail is held within a sphere, behind a veil; it is not quite visible to the Emperor. It stands on a box inscribed with the sign Aries and the sun/moon symbols, representing union.

The card of the Emperor is associated with the astrological sign Aries, the ram. Aries is the first sign of the zodiac; it represents new beginnings and cycles. It is the sign of the initiator, the pioneer, and the masculine impulse. Aries is ruled by the god Mars, the warrior god, ready to do battle. Aries rules the head. The Arian Emperor has vision and loves accepting challenges. The danger lies in the Emperor being so uncompromising that he misses the object of the quest, the Grail. Joseph Campbell states, "It is out of the depth of the unconscious that the energies of life come to us. This cauldron (Grail) is the inexhaustible source, the center, the bubbling spring from which all life proceeds."[7]

The Grail is our connection to the Divine. It holds all that has been known and all that will be known to human consciousness. The Emperor looks after us; he represents our solid foundations. We rely on him to remain constant, to do battle when our security is threatened. He is the part of us that gives us the self-discipline to organize our lives. It is his energy that enables us to make clear decisions and accept life's challenges.

On the Kabbalistic Tree of Life, the Emperor walks the fifteenth path, between Chokmah – wisdom, and Tiphareth – beauty, along the path of Heh, meaning window, incoming light and illumination. The Emperor embodies the divine laws of the universe.

Divinatory Meaning

When the card of the Emperor appears in a spread, it indicates a need for discipline in some area of our lives. One may be asked to initiate a project or be asked to use our organizational skills. Father issues or men in authority may come into focus. We might be reminded not to become too rigid in our opinions or too overbearing in our attitudes. We may have to take charge and control our own lives. We may find ourselves questing for the Grail.

V THE HIEROPHANT

Key words: Listening to the inner voice. Inner tuition. Healing.
Conformity. Beliefs. Learning. Seeking knowledge.

Myth

According to one version of the Greek myth, Chiron was the son
of the Titan god Cronus and the nymph Philyra. One day while
being chased by Cronus, Philyra changed herself into a mare
in order to escape the attention of the amorous god. Cronus
immediately took on the form of a stallion and pursued Philyra.
Mare and stallion mated. In due course Chiron was born, half
man, half horse. Shocked by her son's deformity, Philyra
begged the gods to redeem her from her fate. The gods obliged
and changed her into a linden tree. Chiron's first wound was
the rejection by his mother. Later in the myth, Chiron was

accidentally wounded by one of Hercules's poisoned arrows, inflicting a wound that would not heal. Chiron was both psychologically and physically wounded.

Apollo, Chiron's adoptive father, taught him the knowledge of art, science, divination, and higher wisdom. Athene gave him the gift of reason and the light of knowledge. Chiron then became teacher to many of the Greek heroes.

Chiron made his home in a cave on the dark side of Mount Pelion. Here he practiced his skills in herbalism and healing and became well known for his gifts in surgery and medicine. Yet with all his skills, Chiron could not heal his own wounds. However, as Shaman, he healed others through his own understanding of suffering.

Chiron had both philosophical knowledge and knowledge of the natural laws. In other words, Chiron had connection to the divine and to the manifest; he is often referred to as the Rainbow Bridge between the godhead and the natural world.

While the High Priestess has a knowledge beyond our intellectual capacity, Chiron speaks the High Priestess's wisdom in a language we can all understand if we care to listen. The translation of the title "Hierophant" is the expounder of sacred mysteries.

The cave where Chiron lived was believed to be an entrance to the underworld (the unconscious). Chiron had connection not only to the divine and to the earth, but also to the instinctual realm of the feminine.

Card five indicates the Fool has to balance the divine and the instinctual within himself. He now has the tools to discover his own philosophy and beliefs; he now has enough knowledge to begin to balance traditional doctrine and his own inner doctrine.

The dilemma lies in the Fool's background. He has been taught a doctrine that until this stage of his journey has seemed the only truth. It has never occurred to the Fool before to question the authority of his parent, respected elders, teachers, religious mentors, and political leaders. The Fool has been taught to conform to society's mores. This entails the belief that to be an individual is dangerous, for he could become an outcast in society, be branded a troublemaker, or worse still, be considered crazy. Now the Fool has to learn to become an individual and still live within the boundaries of his community.

In the card of the Hierophant, Chiron's hand is raised in the priestly blessing with two fingers up and two down, indicating hidden and known doctrines. A small sun and moon are on the tips of his index and middle fingers, signifying the union of the God and Goddess. The fingers point to the heavens, surrounded by celestial symbols.

Chiron's face emerges from the clouds. He looks directly at us, soul searching; he is asking if we acknowledge our inner truth. Self-knowledge is the path to healing others and ourselves. In Chiron's other hand lies a key. The key belongs to the High Priestess. She has entrusted that key to Chiron to unlock the minds of those humans who seek knowledge with integrity. Chiron's hand is enclosed by lush, fertile vegetation, suggesting his connection to the natural world. The rainbow is the bridge between earth and the divine.

Traditionally the Hierophant is associated with Taurus. Taurus rules the throat, when the spoken word reflects one's moral code. Chiron is associated with both Sagittarius and Virgo. Sagittarius symbolizes the Quest for personal beliefs and philosophies, teaching and learning. It also has to do with guiding others to find their own inner teacher. Virgo rules the Shaman and healer. Virgo needs to utilize knowledge in the everyday world and to make that knowledge accessible to others.

On the Kabbalistic Tree of Life, the Hierophant walks the sixteenth path between Chokmah Wisdom, the supernal father; and Chesed, mercy, father in manifestation. The Hebrew letter for the Hierophant is Vav, meaning nail or hook. A nail joins things together, fixing one thing to another. It is a symbol of the unity of the divine and the material.

Divinatory Meaning

When the Hierophant appears in a spread, it indicates a time to question what society expects us to believe in the light of what we know is our truth. It could be an opportunity to be honest and retain one's integrity in the face of criticism. The question may arise, "Can I be myself and still function efficiently in society?" One may take on the role of teacher or counselor, or a teacher may appear in your life to impart important knowledge. The healer may appear to heal old wounds. One may be drawn to some new philosophy or spiritual quest.

VI THE LOVERS

Key words: Union. Discrimination. Choices.
Loving relationships. Inner unity.

Myth

The love story of Orpheus and Eurydice, although tragic, holds within it the essence of the Lovers' message which is unity, commitment, and choice.

Orpheus was the son of Apollo and the muse Calliope. Apollo gave his son a musical instrument, a lyre. The boy sang and played so charmingly that he was surrounded by the creatures of the earth, air, and water; wild beasts, birds, and fish. His music was so enchanting that elements of the earth, trees, rocks, and hills also gathered to listen.

Orpheus was in love with Eurydice, and she with him.
Their love was so great they could not bear to be parted.
One day, after their marriage, Eurydice was bitten by a snake
in the grass while trying to escape the advances of the shepherd,
Aristaeus. She died, and Orpheus vowed to win her back from
the gods of the underworld, for he could not live without his
beloved Eurydice.

Orpheus journeyed to the Underworld, approached Hades
and Persephone and sang:

"You Pow'rs, who under Earth your realms extend,
To whom all mortals must one day descend;
If here 'tis granted sacred truth to tell;
I come not curious to explore your Hell;
My wife alone I seek; for her lov'd sake,
These terrors I support, this journey take.

She, luckless wandring, or by fate mis-led,
Chanc'd on a lurking viper's crest to tread;
Thus was she snatch'd untimely to her tomb;
Long I my loss endeavour'd to sustain,
At length I yielded, won by mighty love;
A hope within my heart prevails.

That here, ev'n here, he has been known of old;
At least if truth be by tradition told;
You both by love, and love alone, were join'd.

Now, by the horrors which these realms surround;
Let me again Eurydice receive,
Let Fate her quick-spun thread of life re-weave.

All our possessions are but loans from you,
And soon, or late, you must be paid your due."[8]

As Orpheus sang his lament, the shades and gods alike wept. Their hearts touched, Hades and Persephone agreed Orpheus could take Eurydice back to the light of the upper world, so long as he did not look back at his beloved before reaching their destination.

With great joy, Orpheus led the way with Eurydice behind him. The promise of love returned filled them with happiness. When Orpheus could see the light of day ahead, in his excitement he turned to Eurydice. She was instantly borne away to die a second time. "Farewell," she said, "a last farewell."

> *"But soon, too soon the lover turns his eyes;*
> *Again she falls, again she dies, she dies!*
> *How wilt thou now the fatal sisters move?*
> *No crime was thine, if 'tis no crime to love."*
> *-Alexander Pope*

Orpheus tried again to enter the underworld, but was refused. He wept and grieved; he played a sweet lament. All around him, the animals and trees wept in despair. The Maenads tried to cheer him up, but he refused to join in their mad revelry. Finally they tired of his mournful sobs and tore him limb from limb. Orpheus's ghost entered the underworld a second time, where he was reunited with his beloved Eurydice forever. The choice had been made.

In the card of the Lovers, the couple embrace. They have discovered the delight of sexual union in their own garden of Paradise. The Lovers' garden is fertile, with the High Priestess's pomegranates, the Empress's roses, and the lush colors of life, red and green.

At this stage of his journey the Fool looks to his partner; she is all he sees. He is lost in love and feels this moment will last forever. She, however, looks above to the angel. Somehow she knows their sexual union must encompass the spiritual as well as the physical if their relationship is to last.

In the card, the Lovers form the alchemical pair, usually depicted as the king, the sun god, and the queen, the moon goddess. In Jungian terms, these figures are symbolic of the animus and anima respectively. The positive animus is a woman's magical ideal of man, her Orpheus, her inner man. The positive anima is a man's magical ideal of woman, his Eurydice, his inner woman. So when two people embrace, there are really two sets of twins, the inner and outer couples, the ideal and the real. When the four come together in complete harmony and balanced union, a conjunction is formed. This meeting of opposites is symbolized by the pot of gold in the hands of the angel. The alchemical gold represents wholeness, the complete integration symbolized by sexual union.

Naturally, the Lovers card is associated with the astrological sign Gemini, the twins. Gemini is always searching for the missing twin, the soul-mate. Of all the astrological signs, Gemini is the most restless. Gemini people can be changeable, flirtatious, and fickle; they are searching for the inner twin. Like butterflies they flit from one situation to another hoping to find their other half. Duality is inherent in the sign Gemini. The mythological twins, Apollo, the sun god; and his sister Artemis, the moon goddess, mimic this duality as they perform their monthly dance through the heavens. They begin the dance at the new moon when they are united. During the cycle the goddess moves further and further away from the god until at the full moon she mirrors his magnificence. As the cycle progresses, she moves toward him once more to form a conjunction. The Twins' coming together and separation describes the dilemma of Gemini, whose ultimate goal is to integrate the opposites within the self.

The Lovers walk the seventeenth path on the Kabbalistic Tree of Life from Binah – understanding, to Tiphareth – beauty. This path connects Binah, where energies and knowledge form, to the central focus of manifestation, Tiphareth. Sun and moon consciousness are united on this path. It is a path of choice, discrimination and communication. When on the seventeenth path, we hold our destiny in our own hands. The Hebrew letter is Zain, or Sword, which symbolizes discrimination, which is a very important quality on this path, as it is in matters of love.

Divinatory Meaning

When the card of the Lovers appears in a spread, an important choice will have to be made, usually regarding a relationship. The Fool has reached a crossroad on his journey. His choice now dictates the path he must follow, he cannot stay were he is; a decision must be reached.

This choice is not an easy one. There are usually some complications, especially if the choice involves a relationship. The Fool must learn to discriminate between lust and love; he must also know whether he is ready for union with another with all its implications.

When you draw this card, a new love may enter your life, or an existing relationship may take on a new dimension. You may be challenged to be clear with yourself: What do you want from this relationship? Are you being honest about your needs and desires? Do you love yourself enough to love another as an equal? If a new love enters your life now, it will be an important one; one that could change your direction in life.

Choices involving your individuality within a relationship may arise. For instance, you might be in the position of having to choose between what you want and what your partner wants. Feelings of duty, convenience, or even inertia could affect your judgment. However, with this card, you must remember that you and your needs are important. There are ways to be self-expressive and still retain good relationships.

Sometimes when this card appears a decision needs to be made in an area of your life other than your relationship. A situation or event may require that you think carefully and make your choice from the heart. Sometimes the Lovers card indicates inner unity. You may be feeling balanced and comfortable within yourself.

VII THE CHARIOT

**Key words: Victory. Control. Willpower. Self-mastery.
Overcoming fear. Movement.**

Myth

The people of the Old World represented the yearly cycle of
decay and renewal through their god, who died each year and
was resurrected. Sometimes these gods were symbolic of the
physical sun and its yearly transit. The sun's path through the
sky marked the changing seasons. Even on a daily basis the sun
was seen to be born each morning from Mother Night, lived for
the day, and returned to her womb at sunset. There were many
names for these gods, but their underlying myth was the same.

Hercules, which means "Glory of Hera," was such a god. He
represented the sacred king of early Hellenic Greece, consort of

a tribal nymph, the moon goddess incarnate. Hercules was a solar king and hero who "died" and rose again like the sun. He was associated with the Babylonian hero Gilgamesh.

The twelve labors of Hercules were a representation of the sun's journey through the zodiac. It was as the hero of these twelve labors that Hercules was most honored throughout Greece. On completion of these arduous tasks, Hercules was granted immortality by the gods.

The son of Zeus and Alcmene, Hercules was begotten by Zeus when he assumed the shape of Alcmene's husband and lay with her while her husband was away doing battle. When the child was due to be born, Zeus boasted that the child born before nightfall would become High King. Hera, Zeus's wife, was so enraged by her husband's infidelity that she used her powers to prolong Alcmene's labor, so that another child was born at the appointed time.

Zeus then made Hera agree that after twelve seemingly impossible labors, Hercules would become a god. Later, Zeus tricked Hera by sending Hermes with the newborn child to Olympus, where he put the baby to the sleeping Hera's breast so that her divine milk would give Hercules godlike strength. Hera awoke; as she drew back in horror, milk spurted from her breast and created the Milky Way, the path for the solar hero's journey through the zodiac.

Hera never gave up her quest for revenge; she created all manner of dangers and difficulties throughout Hercules's life. At the end of the story, Hercules dies a martyr. Hermes and Iris conducted him to Olympus where, after a reconciliation with Hera, he married Hebe, the daughter of Hera and Zeus.

In the card of the Chariot, the solar hero, through sheer will and determination, drives his apparently immovable chariot. The charioteer represents the self in Jungian psychology. "The Chariot itself, the body carrying the mind."[9]

The hero's belt has the astrological signs inscribed on it, reflecting his solar journey through the zodiac. On his shoulders, he wears two crescent moons, which symbolize his original association with the moon goddess and the sign Cancer. His breastplate shows Khepri, the Egyptian Scarab god, representing the rising sun and symbolizing the renewal of life and the idea of eternal existence.

The Fool wears laurel leaves around his waist, but the hero wears them about his head, indicating it is through the intellect that the hero claims victory. The canopy above his head is symbolic of Hera's milk, the Milky Way, and of his yearly celestial cycle. Four pillars, each displaying the symbols and colors of the alchemical elements, support the canopy.

The chariot is made of stone, denoting the physical universe. The hero is encased in this stone from the hips down, indicating he has control over his instinctual and sexual nature; he moves forward through reason, logic, and willpower. The hero is sexually mature. He is aware of the power of sexual union and carries the masculine square and the feminine triangle atop his sceptre. The yoni/lingam symbol of sexual union adorns his chariot.

The hero has no reins to direct his chariot; instead, he relies on his strength and conscious will to control chaos. The hero has charge over his feelings, but knows he must be aware of getting stuck if he allows reason alone to rule without heart.

The light and dark sphinxes, who drive the chariot, are the two aspects of the goddess (the feminine), who propel the hero on his journey. The hero must keep in balance and acknowledge the light and dark feminine within himself. In Hercules's city of birth, the sphinx-moon goddess was responsible for the changing seasons. She had the head of a woman, the body of a winged lioness, and the tail of a serpent. In the card, the tails of the two sphinxes are intertwined, symbolic of the goddess's reluctance to be split into either light or dark when she is both. The wings are symbolic of her divinity; the watery unconscious is under her feet.

The card of the Chariot is associated with the astrological sign Cancer. During Hercules's second labor, he encountered and killed a many-headed monster, the Hydra. While the battle raged, Hera encouraged a crab to bite the hero on the foot. Hercules duly crushed the crab, and Hera, to show her appreciation of the crab's action, placed it in the heavens as the astrological constellation, Cancer.[10]

Cancer rules the emotions. The card of the Chariot indicates when we need to be strong and control the emotions in order to find solutions. Cancer and the moon are synonymous with the past and deep-seated emotional memories. The Chariot symbolizes times when we need to put the past behind us and forge ahead.

The hero walks the eighteenth path on the Kabbalistic Tree of Life, between Binah, the great mother, understanding, and Geburah, severity. The path retains balance and a feeling of stability. The symbols are designed to give the soul a feeling of protection. The Hebrew letter is Cheth, meaning fence, which protects, as the shell of the crab protects.

Divinatory Meaning

When the card of the Chariot appears in a spread, it indicates we have the choice to be in charge of our feelings in order to move forward. If we let our emotions get out of control, we cannot make a positive move. Now the Fool is adult and can make decisions.

The Hero in the Chariot card is in a state of tension; he cannot sustain that energy for long. The time has come to use his will-power in an emotional situation. You may find that instead of just coping, you now have the energy to overcome fears, and move on to victory. Inertia and inner conflict are negative aspects of the Chariot. It is time to exercise mind over matter. On a mundane level, the Chariot can indicate one's mode of transport, or moving from one place to another, perhaps moving home.

VIII STRENGTH

**Key words: Strength. Courage. Compassion. Self-confidence.
Love. Gentleness. Overcoming fears. Forgiveness.**

Myth

The Babylonian goddess Ishtar was the divine personification
of the planet Venus, and was also a moon goddess. She had a
dual personality. She is sometimes depicted as the Divine Love
Goddess, with a ring in her left hand, and the cup of love and
plenty in her right. At other times, she is shown armored like
the warrior goddess Athene. Ishtar was seen in her duality
as mother holding her breasts (symbolic of generosity and
fertility), and as virgin warrior. "Virgin" here is used not in
the sense of chastity but to denote the integrated feminine.

Lions were sacred to Ishtar. In the old sculptures, she stands on her chariot, drawn by seven lions, with a bow in her hands, ready to do battle. Ishtar was also the sexual woman, always on the lookout for a new lover.[11] She had many opposing attributes; she could be tender and loving, as well as irritable and violent.

Ishtar was a later, more complex goddess than her predecessor, the gentle Innana, although their myths are similar. Both loved a seasonal god, who died and was reborn each year. Like Innana, Ishtar descended to the underworld in search of her dead lover, knowing she would have to face her dark sister, Ereshkigal. When the gates of the underworld would not open immediately, Ishtar became enraged. She threatened to break the lock and tear down the gates of Hell; she threatened to use her powers to raise the dead. However, Ishtar soon learned she would not succeed by using unbridled violence.

As she descended into the underworld, Ishtar was forced to give up a garment at each of the seven gates of hell, until she was stripped of all the power her finery symbolized. She stood before her dark sister Erishkigal condemned to death; she was hung upon a peg like a rotting piece of meat and there she remained until the gods intervened. The land and all life, mourning the goddess's absence, had become barren, so the gods had to ensure her return. Her wish granted, Ishtar regained her garments at each of hell's seven gates, and re-emerged into the upper world with her lover. The mighty Ishtar was forced to subdue her lion nature, in the presence of her own dark sister, Erishkigal, the mirror of herself.

In the card of Strength, Ishtar sits astride a lion, which represents her pride and ego. The symbol of the lion is one of the oldest and richest in meaning. Its relationship to gold and the sun has made it an emblem of gods and royalty. In alchemy, gold was called the lion of metals, and is the masculine principle of vigor and strength.[12] In the Strength card, Ishtar is subduing her lion nature, her passionate ego-driven instincts;

she is in charge. Ishtar has grown to love all parts of her personality. She loves her wild animal side, but does not want her instincts to gain dominance over her connection to the divine, symbolized by the lemniscate above her head. The duality of her nature is balanced. The white dress is a traditional symbol of the bride and chastity. Ishtar is bride to the lion; she has married the different parts of herself to make a unified whole. She is chaste in the sense that she has honored and integrated both the dark and the light sides of her personality; she is "one-unto-herself."

Ishtar wears the laurel leaves about her waist, signifying her victory over unbridled instincts. She also wears the Empress's red roses in her mane as a crown, indicating she does not negate her sensuality in favor of the intellect. The white and red roses are symbolic of the virginal and sexually mature aspects of the goddess; they also signify her capacity to love. The arched date palms are sacred to Ishtar. They signify her fertile abundance and connection to the earth.

The card of Strength is associated with the astrological sign Leo, a masculine fiery sign, ruled by the sun. The Leo nature is generous, loving, and proud, but like the lion, it may need taming. Otherwise, arrogance and false pride could become the dominant aspect.

Astrology is believed to have originated in Babylon, Ishtar's kingdom. At that time, around 3,800 B.C.E., the virgin (Virgo) was identified with Ishtar, the love goddess. Every 2,000 years, the sun rises in an earlier sign, so that over the centuries, the tail of the lion entered the virgin's place in the heavens; hence the goddess's title of "Oura," the lion's tail. Gradually the lion's body followed, until eventually the sign of the virgin had a lion's body with the head of the virgin – an appropriate image for the card of Strength.[13]

Strength walks the nineteenth path on the Kabbalistic Tree of Life, between Chesed – mercy, and Geburah – severity. Realizations are profound on this path. This is the end result of the experience and understanding of the cycle of evolution.

On the highest level, the test is the ability to face everything that has happened during the complete cycle of personal evolution. There is a great sense of inevitability on this path; you need to face your destiny with courage, faith, vision, and discrimination.

The Hebrew letter is Teth, meaning serpent, which is represented by the Tantric image of the female serpent, coiled in the lowest Chakra of the human body, in the pelvis. The rising of the Kundalini serpent to the brain creates a state of bliss, as union with the Divine is experienced. The Kundalini is the life force, how we harness this force expresses our evolution.

Divinatory Meaning

When the card of Strength appears in a spread, you will have the strength to overcome those parts of yourself you do not need any more. The Fool has faced passions he never knew he had until now. Now he has the strength to calm the inner beast (his anger, lust, and false pride) with self-love and forgiveness. A situation may arise where you will have the confidence to say, "I can do this, I can *deal with* this situation, not just cope." The card of Strength is about having inner power, being able to forgive, and accepting our own faults. It is also about having compassion for others, who have not yet faced their own shadows. You will be filled with optimism and faith, enabling you to overcome difficult situations with love and gentleness, not force. You will be able to resolve problems now, if you respect others' opinions, while not wavering from your convictions, if they come from the heart.

IX   THE HERMIT

Key words: Wisdom. Inner counseling. Completion.
Guide. Self-knowledge. Solitude. Self-sufficiency.

Myth

In Greek mythology, Hestia/Vesta was the eldest child of
the Titans, Cronus and Rhea. Cronus swallowed his children
as they were born, after it was predicted that one of his progeny
would de-throne him. Vesta, being the eldest, was the first to
be swallowed. When the last of Rhea's children was born, she
tricked Cronus by wrapping a stone in swaddling. Cronus
swallowed the stone and the baby, Zeus, grew up in hiding
only to overthrow his father as predicted.

Zeus retrieved his siblings who had been devoured. Vesta,
the first to be swallowed, was the last to be disgorged. It was

she who spent the longest time in solitude, imprisoned within her father's belly. Vesta symbolizes the times when we need to reflect, to go within. She represents patience and understands the meaning of time.

In mythology, Vesta was withdrawn from the material world. She kept a low profile, not becoming involved in the intrigues and exploits of the other gods and goddesses. There are no known statues of Vesta, but we know she was greatly venerated in ancient times, and was worshiped as the spirit of the flame that burned in the central hearth in every Greek/Roman household. Although unseen, Vesta was the focus of the home. The flame, central to the family, is the flame within ourselves, the inner guide to peace and wisdom.

The archetype of the Hermit is also represented by the Celtic figure, the old veiled one. A very old deity known by many names, she appears as the guide, helper or hinderer. She is known as the wise crone, who guards the magical cauldron. When the Fool, as Perceval, is seeking the Grail, it is the Hermit who, first scolds him for his mistakes, then guides him to the culmination of his quest, the Grail.

The Hermit cannot teach or lead others to the secrets of life, until she has lived, has known aloneness, solitude, and pain, and has experienced the many rich memories of merely being alive.

In the card of the Hermit, Vesta, the wise one, holds her lantern aloft, illuminating the way for the Fool and for us on our journey. The six-pointed star is formed by two triangles: an upward, masculine, fire triangle, and the downward-pointing feminine, water triangle, symbolizing unity of soul and spirit. The Hermit's light is for everyone who seeks truth and knowledge. In her other hand, the Hermit holds the Serpent of Enlightenment, who guards the secrets of death and re-renewal. On her breast is the eternal flame of Vesta. The Fool meets his teacher and guide. The Hermit enables him to understand the meaning of time, and the natural cycle of life. For the first time, the Fool acknowledges his mortality. The Hermit stands on a windswept mountain peak; she is close to spirit, the stark landscape symbolizing seclusion and withdrawal from worldly ways. The Hermit's bare feet indicate her connection to Mother Nature. A flock of birds disappears into the clouds, symbolizing the transient cycles, seasons, and time.

The Hermit is associated with the astrological sign Virgo, the virgin. As the continuity of life was symbolized by Vesta's flame, it was kept alive and tended by Vesta's priestesses, the vestal virgins. We need to tend and keep our own inner flame alive by self-knowledge and self-sufficiency. Virgo has rulership over the everyday routine of life. Vesta is there to guide us daily; she teaches us to meditate and to discriminate. She teaches us how to manage the stresses of life. Vesta is where we have the ability to center ourselves.

The Hermit walks the twentieth path on the Kabbalistic Tree of Life, from Chesed – mercy, to Tiphareth – beauty. On this path, we can release energies that create opportunities to explore the teachings of all those who brought knowledge to humankind. "I am ready to accept change on this path." We are becoming more certain of what is real. The Hebrew letter is Yod, meaning the open hand, a symbol of giving and receiving and a symbol of beginnings. On this path, we can become new people.

Divinatory Meaning

When the Hermit appears in a spread, it means turning your back on the physical world for the present, so that inner work can take place. This is in preparation for the change which comes when we reach the Wheel of Fortune. You may need to be left alone, to experience that which is meaningful and significant to you. It may be a time to review your journey so far: what have you learned about yourself? By seeking inner counseling, the answers will come. You know what you want. Allow Vesta to guide you to self-knowledge.

X THE WHEEL OF FORTUNE

**Key words: Change. Opportunity. Expansion.
Openness. Flexibility. Movement. Risking. Taking chances.**

Myth

The Moirae, also known as the Fates, were the triple goddesses of fate and destiny. They were analogous with the Erinyes (the Furies), Alecto, Tisiphone, and Megaera, fearsome avengers who defended the matrilineal line and kept social order. They punished severely anyone who committed a crime against that order, including the crime of excessive pride (hubris). For the guilty, there was no escaping their wrath.

Their counterparts, the Moirae, were the spinners of destiny. These Triple Fates were Clotho, the Spinner, the young crescent phase of the moon trinity who spins the thread of life; Lachesis, disposer of lots, the mature full moon phase goddess who determines life's length; and Atropos, inflexibility, the waning dark moon phase who cuts life's thread at death.

In one version of the myth, the Furies were born of the drops of blood from the castrated sky god Uranus, which fell down to fertilize Mother Earth. Another myth says the Furies were born out of Mother Night, necessity, and are older than time. Necessity, time, and fate are interwoven into the fabric of life. All the gods, even Zeus, were bound by their decree.

Fate and destiny have always been seen as feminine, as women hold the secrets of life within their bodies. Similarly, spinning and weaving are seen as female occupations. The goddess of fate is seen spinning the web of life, the cycle of time.

The ancient Greeks had a theory that everything and everyone had a place and function, and an allotted space in time. Those who sought to raise themselves above their station in life, or became arrogant about their personal importance, were demonstrating a lack of humility before the gods. The worst possible sin was hubris, or false pride. Those who tried to escape the course of destiny attracted the punitive attentions of the Furies.

A modern example is the Olympic athlete, already a hero, who, lacking faith in himself, the gods, and the course of destiny, takes performance-enhancing drugs to achieve success. In doing so, he defies the social order. Retribution follows in the form of exposure, ridicule, and public disgrace.

In the card of the Wheel of Fortune, the Triple Moirae spin, measure, and are ready to cut. They belong to the Great Cosmic Round of which we are all a part. We are each born at a particular time, which is entirely individual, and sets us apart from everyone else, as reflected in the natal horoscope, the blueprint of life. This blueprint contains all the talents, potential gifts, and challenges we are destined to meet during life.

We have free will to accept or deny these seemingly fated opportunities when they appear in the form of an event, a person, or a gift. At other times we get swept along by a chain of events over which we have no control. There is really only one surety, that at the end of life we will confront Atropos; our physical body must die, on that we can rely. However, according to myth, it is not only mere mortals who must give the Fates their due.

The Wheel of Fortune is associated with the planet Jupiter/Zeus. Jupiter is considered the planet of expansion and growth, opportunities, new horizons, and the quest to extend and expand our knowledge, vision, and understanding. In the myth even Zeus is answerable to the Fates. The negative aspect of Jupiter is to overextend in any area of life. Overindulgence, overdoing anything could attract the attention of the Furies.

The Wheel of Fortune is found on the twenty-first path, on the Kabbalistic Tree of Life, connecting Chesed – mercy, and Netzach – victory. This path is one of choice. Something comes up unexpectedly; one can take it up, or let it slide by unnoticed. This path can lead to selfless activities that can help others, and creates circumstances that helps us find our way to the Grail, our spiritual essence, and how to manifest it in our life. Our choice is to hear the call or not.

The Hebrew letter for this path is Kaph, the palm of the hand, symbolizing the guides who help us on our journey.

Divinatory Meaning

When the Wheel of Fortune appears in a spread, it indicates change, and suggests going with the natural cycle of life, both inner and outer. It also indicates a need to be flexible and open to new opportunities that will appear now. It is a time to question whether you are a victim of your fate, or whether you grab an opportunity and use it to advantage. Changes in your life that occur now could bring about benefits and rewards. The Wheel turns; be observant, look for the small indicators that could lead to the big changes.

XI JUSTICE

**Key words: Balance. Action/reaction. Truth.
Fairness. Adjustment. Legalities. Responsibility.**

Myth

Maat is the Egyptian goddess of truth and justice. She
weighed a feather against the heart of a dead person. If the
scales balanced, the person would know happiness in the
after-life, living side-by-side with the gods. If the person's
heart was heavy with evil deeds, he or she was devoured by
the monstrous goddess Ahemait. Maat was worshiped in the
rhythm of truth. In Greek mythology, Themis is the goddess of
truth and justice. She was the personification of the divine law
or right which ought to control all human affairs; she judged all
humanity. Themis lived on Mt. Olympus, and descended to

earth during the battle of the Titans, remaining there throughout the golden age of Greece. She taught humankind the laws of right and moderation until the bronze age, when men fell into degradation. When violence and greed dominated the people, and their desires became unbalanced with the laws of life, Themis turned her back on humanity and returned to Olympus. The gods, including Zeus, consulted and acted on the advice of Themis. She was always honored on Mt. Olympus, and was the first wife of Zeus. Even after he married Hera, Themis was always at Zeus's side, offering advice and service.

In the card of Justice, Themis/Maat, is staring out with unflinching gaze. Ancient artists portrayed her with open staring eyes; the modern artist usually covers her eyes. Perhaps blind Justice suggests the law's impartiality; or perhaps Themis ruled prophecy and could look into the hearts of men, and we became so afraid of her retribution that we sought to escape her divine laws by covering those searching eyes.

Justice carries an upright sword in one hand and scales in the other, indicating the severity and accuracy of her judgment. A serpent is coiled around her arm. The serpent is sacred to the goddess, and indicates the law is feminine in gender. It was from Themis that Zeus derived his judicial authority.[14]

The all-seeing eye is fixed at the throat of Justice; she sees and speaks the truth. Behind her, a peacock's iridescent tail feather eyes symbolize the star-filled night sky, and the goddesses' watchfulness. They are her plumes of justice, against which the hearts of men were weighed.[15]

Justice sits, stern, and immovable; she will not waver from her karmic laws of cause and effect. Justice teaches us to judge our actions and know the results. Everything must be balanced: night and day, sleep and wakefulness. We learn to take responsibility for our actions and can expect rewards for good deeds, punishment for bad.

Justice is associated with the astrological sign Libra, the scales. The key word for Libra is harmony in all things, especially in relationships. The typical Libran is accused of procrastination.

This may be because the Libran sees all sides of an issue and tries to bring all opposing elements into balance, to create a harmonious whole, while still being fair, weighing and rationalizing everything.

Libra is the first sign above the horizon in the horoscope. That means it is the first sign away from being individual; it incorporates others as equals. The Libran has to balance his or her own desires against the desires of an equal, just like the scales, weighing and measuring, action and reaction.

The Justice card is ruled by the element air. At this stage of the journey, balance comes from the intellect, not the heart.

Justice walks the twenty-second path on the Kabbalistic Tree of Life, between Geburah – severity, and Tiphareth – beauty. On this path we leave the security of Tiphareth and face karmic adjustments. This path reveals the duality of our nature, the good and the bad. We learn to recognize that we are human with human failings. We learn to forgive those failings. By being faithful to our spiritual truth, we will receive a fair and just outcome in any situation. The Hebrew letter is Lamed, which means ox goad; we are driven to fulfill our destiny.

Divinatory Meaning

When the card of Justice appears in a spread, it is a time to be responsible for your actions. Do your actions reflect your desires? Are you being free and honest with yourself? Or are you just going along with the crowd to keep harmony? Being balanced is being able to face reality in an objective way. Being honest with oneself requires a great deal of courage and awareness; being honest and open with others, even more. Nothing can change if you cannot make up your mind. Sometimes the scales must be tipped a little in favor of the feather, other times in favor of the heart. However, the Justice card is about moderation, so do not become too rigid, self-critical, and judgmental about yourself if the scales waver slightly. After all, we are only human. If you can perform the actions you have been putting off, put your words into practice, and take responsibility for that area of your life you have been avoiding, the scales are fairly balanced. Relationship decisions may come up. You may have to weigh and measure the value of a relationship; how you feel versus what you think. Sometimes the Justice card can relate to legal issues or your concept of what is fair and just in a particular situation. You may have to make an important decision that requires an unbiased open mind. Remember, Justice can negotiate.

XII THE HANGED MAN

Key words: Surrender. Acceptance. Patience. Faith. Trust.
Repetitive patterns. Sacrifice. Higher understanding.

Myth

Dionysus was a god of sacrifice in ancient and classical Greek mythology. He was worshiped as the sacred king whom the goddess ritually killed with a thunderbolt in the seventh month from the winter solstice, and whom her priestesses devoured.[16] Sometimes a bull representing Dionysus was cut into pieces and sacrificed to the goddess. This ritual happened yearly to ensure the fertility of the land. Dionysus was also associated with the goat, and in that form was closely connected with the god Pan.

The Hellenistic Greeks and their god Zeus brought to an end the yearly sacrifice of the sacred king. According to myth, Zeus saved the dismembered infant Dionysus from death by stitching the still-beating heart of the child in his own thigh, and fulfilling the gestation period. Thus Dionysus became the twice-born god.

Dionysus was also a god of all kind of trees, but was especially the god of the vine, wine, and ecstasy. There are many stories and common threads that connect Dionysus to sacrifice, resurrection, and the ecstatic feminine. His priestesses were the Maenads who celebrated his orgies with wild drunkenness, dancing, nakedness, and sacrificial feasting.

Over time, the reputation of Dionysus changed dramatically. Where in earlier times he was seen only as the god of the vine and orgiastic delirium, he later became a symbol of everlasting life, the prototype of Christ. Like Christ, Dionysus died and was resurrected.

In the card of the Hanged Man, Dionysus hangs suspended in time. His suspension is symbolic of our unfilled yearnings and longings. He hangs patiently, from a leafy branch, across the abyss; he is hanging between the past and the future. Dionysus wears a red shirt, the color of life and sacrifice; his black pants, the color of the fertilized winter earth before the spring (rebirth), bear the symbolic emblems of a pine cone, the Thyrsus, and the cross of Christ. Ivy leaves adorn his hair, a traditional connection with Dionysus believed to both cure and intoxicate. The Three Hours watch from the clouds, as the goddesses of the changing seasons. They wait patiently as time passes. Under Dionysus the waters of Lethe (forgetfulness) flow; spirits drank the waters of forgetfulness before being reincarnated. The waters flow on towards the twin mountain peaks of enlightenment, and consciousness, for the Hanged Man trusts in a higher force that he will be fine. A rainbow bridge connects the two rocky cliff faces, symbolic of the Kabbalistic pillars of severity and mercy.

The planet Neptune is associated with the card of the Hanged Man. The key words are sacrifice and surrender of the ego. The negative side of the Hanged Man lies in resisting surrender. We must let go of things that impede growth and self-realization.

The things we are being asked to surrender are no longer necessary. Old established ideas and instilled standards need revision. What was important in the past may be blocking us from new exciting experiences.

The Hanged Man symbolizes sacrifice of the old skeletons in the cupboard, the old hurtful and painful experiences that keep us in the mode of victim and martyr. Sometimes we project these roles onto others in order to become the Savior. Neptune is the planet of illusion and disillusion. Like the Hanged Man, sometimes we may need to turn ourselves upside-down to see the truth in a situation. To face reality and look at ourselves and situations from a different perspective can be very revealing.

On the Kabbalistic Tree of Life, the Hanged Man walks the twenty-third path, between Geburah, severity, and Hod, splendour. On this path, we leave the lower understanding of Hod, to reach the higher understanding of Geburah. Here, we have the ability to change our viewpoint for something different. This path teaches tolerance and enlightenment and releases the desire to merge with universal forces. While we are hanging there, we will hear the word of god; we are waiting for enlightenment. The Hebrew letter is Mem, meaning water, which symbolizes love and life; without water, there is no existence.

Divinatory Meaning

When the Hanged Man appears in a spread, you are being asked to surrender some part of yourself; old patterns of behavior, addictions, old outworn ways of thinking. The Hanged Man cannot move while suspended between the past and the future; he has to look to the present. Denial of attitudes and hanging on to obsessive habits keep you in suspension. What are you being asked to surrender? Perhaps you need to look at the situation in a new light. The Hanged Man requires patience and tolerance. Sometimes a time of waiting is required for you to recognize the repetitive pattern in your life. However, the Hanged Man cannot hang there in suspended time forever. Change will come when you learn to have enough faith and trust in yourself to let go.

XIII DEATH

Key words: Transformation, Death/Rebirth-birth.
Letting go. Endings. Release. Detachment. New forms.

Myth

In the Greek myth, the gods Hades and Persephone had
sovereignty over the underworld. It was believed the infernal
region was situated at the center of the earth, where the rivers
Acheron, river of sadness, Cocytus, river of lamentation, Lethe,
river of forgetfulness, and the river Styx flowed. Before the
gates of Hades could be reached, the soul had to pass through
the grove of Persephone, where black poplars and sterile
willows grew.

Hades did not get involved in the problems of humanity or
the intrigues of the other gods. He kept very much to himself,

and has only been sighted twice in the upper world. The purpose of one of the visits was to rape and abduct the fair Persephone. Demeter, Persephone's mother and goddess of the grain, was distraught. She had lost her beloved daughter; she searched for her, she grieved, but no one seemed to know what had happened to her child. After a long time, and much effort on Demeter's part, Hecate and the sun god, Helios confessed they had witnessed the crime. Demeter, angry, threw the world into deep famine. Nothing would grow; the world and all her creatures were dying. Zeus was forced to negotiate with Hades for Persephone's return. However, Persephone had eaten a pomegranate seed, the food of the dead, which bound her to Hades and the underworld forever. As a compromise, it was agreed that Persephone was to spend half the year in the upper world with her mother, and the other half in the underworld with her husband, Hades.

Each spring, Persephone was personified in the new green growth of the season. This symbolizes the way we surface and are re-born after spending time in our own underworld of grief, for the loss of a loved one, the breakdown of a relationship or other profound loss. This is the cyclic process: we are born, live and die many times during one lifetime.

When autumn had shed her leaves and the harvest had been reaped, Persephone returned to the underworld and her husband. We return to the darkness because we have lost our way temporarily and have fallen victim to feelings of depression and despair. Persephone's name means "she who destroys light." As we descend, there is no light. Hades' Roman name, Pluto, means riches; if we descend to the unconscious realm willingly, we reap the riches to be found there, the reward of self-knowledge.

Persephone is the virgin aspect of the triple moon goddess. Demeter symbolizes the full moon phase, and Hecate, the waning dark moon phase. In the card of Death, Hecate, conductor of souls, is there to ferry us across the river Styx to Queen Persephone's realm. Hecate casts her nets; gathering up lost souls, she holds the silver threads of life to which we cling, too afraid to let go. Hecate is the reaper of the harvest after life has ceased to prosper. She cuts down that which is no longer important or useful in our lives so that new shoots may flourish.

The tattered sail in the card reminds us that all life is transient. Some situations have to die; old attachments could keep us from new opportunities. The waning dark moon is in the sky, a figure rises up in the process of re-birth. Transformation takes place as the waning moon soon changes to a new moon, and the promise of rejuvenation and renewal.

The astrological sign Scorpio is associated with the card of death. Scorpio is closely linked to the themes of death, re-birth and transformation. Some Scorpios see living as a series of deaths and re-births. Ruled by the element water, Scorpio knows the very depths of emotional feelings, and is inherently connected to the great mysteries of life. Scorpio is a sign of merging and blending with a partner, and at the same time being painfully aware of feeling separate. That is why some Scorpio people find that intense relationships send them to the underworld and keep them there.

Death walks the twenty-fourth path on the Kabbalistic Tree of Life, between Tiphareth, beauty, and Netzach, victory. On this path we leave the desire nature of Netzach, and enter the light of the sun. We leave behind the things we think we need; this is the path of acceptance, of what we must be. If there is to be change, something must die. The Hebrew letter is Nun, meaning fish, which symbolizes life. On the twenty-fourth path, death has to be accepted before higher consciousness and renewed life can be achieved.

Divinatory Meaning

When Death appears in a spread, it indicates that something in your life has come to the end of its cycle; be prepared to let it die. There is no point dwelling on resentment and rage, on "what ifs," or resenting a loss that cannot be retrieved. We must grieve and mourn our losses with the knowledge and confidence that new life always replaces the old; it is part of life's cycle. When Death appears, it does not mean physical death, it symbolizes total transformation in some area of your life. Hecate is honored at the crossroads; you have now reached a crossroad in your life. How will you honor her? Will you be willing to forgo old attachments, like old friends who no longer nourish you, or an old lover you no longer love, but hang onto out of habit? What will you do about an occupation or life-style that no longer excites you? Now is the opportunity to accept the inevitable change, making way for the new.

XIV TEMPERANCE

Key words: Balance. Vision. Moderation. Tempering. Bringing gifts and talents together to create something of value.

Myth

Iris, goddess of the rainbow, was messenger of the gods, especially to the goddess Hera. Iris lived on Mt. Olympus; her main function was to convey divine messages to humankind. Like her counterpart, Hermes, she was sometimes seen carrying the magical staff, the Caduceus. Iris, like Hermes, could travel from the upper worlds to the lower worlds with ease. She was responsible for the fertilizing rain which nourished the earth; her rainbow was seen as the goddess descending to earth forming a bridge between earth and sky.

In the card of Temperance, the winged goddess, Iris, is symbolic of the alchemical union of opposites, like the mixing and blending of her many colors. The divine water flowing between the feminine silver cup and the masculine golden cup is the water of life, carefully poured back and forth with never a drop wasted. The silver and gold cups are also symbolic of the moon and sun, night and day.

Temperance is the alchemist. Her art is in transmuting base metals into silver and gold; she takes the fragmented parts of us, the good and the bad, and blends them into something of worth. Temperance takes chaotic matter and creates form, blending the elements, air, water, fire, and earth. With the grace of the god and goddess, Temperance creates life.

In the card of Temperance, Iris is represented as the middle pillar on the Tree of Life. Directly above her lies the path of the High Priestess, and above that lies Kether the crown, the spark of all existence. On the middle path, all things are united in perfect harmony. Iris's right foot is in the watery world of Yesod, the feminine, unconscious realm of dreams, and the imagination. Her other foot is on the path that leads to the sun and Tiphareth, the realm of realization and beauty. On either side of Iris are the twin towers of Binah, the great mother (the Empress); and Chokmah, the great father (the Emperor). These powerful forces are united and illuminated by the light of the sun. Under Iris's feet lies the path to Malkuth, where all things manifest in the real world, and our dreams take on form, become solid.

Temperance is associated with the astrological sign, Sagittarius. Sagittarius is a fiery masculine sign; it symbolizes vision, the quest for higher knowledge beyond the ordinary boundaries of human thought. Its highest aim is to find enlightenment. Sagittarius is represented as the centaur, half man, half horse, which is the marriage of the natural world and man's quest for consciousness. The centaur aims his arrow high into the heavens; to him, anything is possible. There are no limits; that is why the Sagittarian can outdo himself by overstepping the mark. Temperance is about balance and moderation. When the balance is tipped, the arrow is lost in the great cosmos of words and unreal optimism. Sagittarius is ruled by the god Zeus/Jupiter, who never did things by half measure. Sagittarius has the spiritual warrior energy, so his vision is a bright optimistic one, enabling him to confront the Devil card which comes next on the journey.

Temperance walks the twenty-fifth path, on the Kabbalistic Tree of Life, from Tipareth – beauty, to Yesod – foundation. The key words are integration and balance on the middle pillar. The journey on this path is the outward quest to find our place in the world, whilst inner transmutation is taking place. This in turn changes our soul, hence changes reality. When we ascend the Tree, our soul aspires to higher consciousness, sustained only by one recourse, faith. On the descent of the Tree, we experience a downpouring of light and love, to the individuals seeking to make contact with what really sustains us. The Hebrew letter is Samech, meaning prop or staff, the magical staff of Hermes and Iris or the healing staff of Asclepius. The prop represents the faith we have in something higher that sustains us on this path.

Divinatory Meaning

When Temperance appears in a spread, it indicates a period of feeling balanced within yourself. You are able to fulfill your dreams, whether in relationship, in a special project or just feeling good about yourself. You have the ability to make things manifest, keeping one foot on the ground, while allowing divine energy to inspire you. Temperance is about unity and integration. It is a card of balance, but it is unlike the balance represented by the card of Justice, where balance is gained through reason and critical judgment. Temperance is the harmonious blending of the light and the dark sides of ourselves into a whole. Temperance suggests the need to think things through carefully and ask the questions: "What am I trying to balance in my life now? What areas of my life are in conflict? What changes need to be made to create harmony? Are my relationships one-sided? Am I giving top priority to others when I need something for myself?" Temperance means taking control of your life.

XV THE DEVIL

**Key words: Bondage. Compulsion. Materialism. Fear.
Illusions. Sexuality. Oppression. Limitation.
Obsession. Depression. Hopelessness.**

Myth

In old Europe there was no god who could equal the goddess
in power or prestige; but she had a lover who was at times the
beneficent "Serpent of Wisdom" and also the beneficent "Star of
Life," her son, Lucifer, whose name means bringer of light. As
the evening star, he led in the light of the moon, was reborn
each year and grew to adulthood as the year advanced. He
destroyed the serpent and won the goddess's heart. Her love
destroyed him, but from his ashes another serpent was born,
which at Easter laid an egg which she ate, so that the Son was
reborn to her once more.[18]

The ancient myth of Lucifer, the light bringer, carried through to Christian texts. Gnostic Christians believed the light brought by Lucifer was true enlightenment. The Bible story supports this belief. In the Garden of Eden, the Lord god cursed the serpent when he knew that Adam had eaten the fruit of the tree of good and evil; and said to his angels: "Behold, the man has become like one of us, knowing good and evil and now, lest he put forth his hand and take also of the tree of life, and eat, and live forever...therefore Yahweh sent him forth from the garden of Eden, to till the ground from which he was taken. He drove out the man; and at the east of the Garden of Eden he placed the cherubim and a flaming sword which turned every way, to guard the way to the tree of life."[19] Lucifer, in the form of a serpent, gave Adam and Eve the apple, and thereby, the light of wisdom which revealed the closely guarded secrets of their heavenly father.[20]

In the card of the Devil, Lucifer wears the green scaly skin of the serpent; his black wings indicate his divine origins. He holds the trident, symbolic of the triple phallus, for the perpetuation of life. The pentacle on his breast also symbolizes life; pointing downward, it represents the head of the horned god in Celtic mythology. Lucifer is relaxed and confident, for his role is to seduce and enlighten us. We are seduced into the traps of fear, hopelessness and despondency. Some of us wallow in melancholy. We try to remain in our individual hells, convincing ourselves we have no avenue of escape. We console ourselves with the seductions of materialism, but the fact remains, we cannot buy our way out of this dilemma. We feel trapped. Lucifer laughs when we succumb to overeating, drinking or other indulgence. Some of us will resort to extremes in order to avoid the pain of self-analysis. In the card, two fig-ures hold up a mirror. They are chained to Lucifer, and have been there so long they have turned to stone. They are in bondage to their limitations, and have chosen to stagnate in their "blinkered" view of life.

In the mirror, a woman has caught a glimpse of reality and she doesn't like what she sees. She wants the image to go away; the light bringer has given her the gift of seeing herself as she really is. Now she can begin to work on all those hidden fears, own her own projections, and face those ego-driven illusions she has, of herself and her world. Lucifer's bribes are attractive, appealing and persistent, he tests how far down the track of compulsive, obsessive desires we will travel before loosening the chains and seeing the light. We must own and acknowledge our chains.

The card of the Devil is associated with the astrological sign Capricorn. Capricorn is an earth sign and is closely linked with the Greek god Pan, who was a fertility god with a very lustful nature. Pan was depicted as goatlike with horns and cloven hooves, the word *panic* is derived from his name (we panic when Lucifer shows his face). Some of the Devil's temptations are lust, insatiable sexuality, and hidden desires.

The goatlike character of Pan is nimble and fond of climbing mountains, like the ambitious Capricorn, who climbs to the top of the executive ladder. While ambition is desirable, it can also produce obsessive behavior, such as the workaholic. Capricorn has the reputation of falling into the clutches of depression and limitation if their ambitions are thwarted. This is an example of the thin line between light and shadow, and how choice, and acceptance of its ultimate consequences, plays such a vital role. Personal power lies in seeing our own hang-ups, only then will the road ahead be clear.

The Devil walks the twenty-sixth path on the Kabbalistic Tree of Life between Tiphareth, beauty, and Hod, splendour. The twenty-sixth path tests the intellect as the soul travels toward the divine. This is a revealing path; cherished illusions and intellectual falsities can be changed. The lesson on this path is to accept a new way of seeing things, for to accept only what our eyes tell us is to be in bondage. The Hebrew letter is Ayin, meaning eye. The only way to see things clearly is with the spiritual eye.

Divinatory Meaning

When the Devil card appears in a spread, light will be thrown
on some area of your life that is keeping you in harness, stopping you from moving ahead. You may find your relationship
is based on lust, not love. A relationship could have all the
earmarks of a fatal attraction or perhaps you realize your
relationship is limiting, offering only material security, and
fear is stopping you from exploring other possibilities. You
may have to examine your attitudes in this material world,
where advertising and the media create illusions about how
we should look, and what we want but do not need. Fear of
not being accepted by others is one of the greatest fears, and
leads to self-destruction and involuntary servitude.

The Devil is there to tempt us. It is through temptation that
we come to know our weaknesses and our strengths. If we
follow the crowd, we never really know ourselves. We blame
every one else for our limitations, believing problems are
always someone else's fault. The questions to ask yourself are,
"In what area of my life am I bound? In what areas am I using
undue control and manipulation? What are my fears that are
holding me back?"

XVI THE TOWER

**Key words: Breakthrough/breakdown. Change. New structure.
Destruction of old forms. Liberation. Upheaval.
Awakening. Shattering. Revelation.**

Myth

Mankind has always been inspired to erect sky-reaching
monuments in an attempt to be closer to their gods. The
preference to build these monoliths out of stone, rather than
clay, meant they would outlast the impermanence of the flesh
and the ravages of time. The Babylonians built the famous
mountain temple, the Ziggurat; the Egyptians built the pyra-
mids. Titan giants pulled up surrounding mountains and piled
them up, one on top of the other, in an attempt to reach the
heavenly Mt. Olympus.

Possibly the last of these monuments were the great Gothic cathedrals, built throughout Europe during the middle ages, with their tall spires soaring heavenward. Today's language includes the words aspire, inspire, and inspiration, referring to a divine connection. In our modern world, we still build tall edifices, but to venerate a different god, the god of materialism, wealth, and power. The Biblical story of the Tower of Babel is symbolically very close in meaning to card number sixteen, the Tower. In the story, god grew angry with the people, who thought they could bridge the gap between earth and sky with their tower. They were duly punished because they tried to elevate their position from being mere mortals to sitting side by side with god. They committed the unforgivable sin of hubris (false pride).

King Acrisius of Argos suffered false pride. The king had only one child, a daughter, Danae. A prophecy had been made that Danae would bear a son, who on reaching adulthood, would destroy his grandfather and take over the kingdom. The king immediately built a tower of bronze (some say a dungeon), and imprisoned his daughter. However, Danae had not escaped the attention of the amorous Zeus, who entered the tower in the form of a shower of gold (the lightning flash) and impregnated Danae. She bore a son, Perseus, as a result of what appeared to be a miraculous conception.

Silly King Acrisius still thought he could trick the gods and stop the wheel of fate from turning. The king sealed Danae and her newborn babe in a wooden ark and cast them adrift on the sea. "Out of sight, out of mind," thought the foolish king. The king denied life; he wanted nothing to change. His megalomaniac need for power created nothing but pain and destruction in the end. The king believed his actions would save him from his fate, but with life cast out, there remained only apathy and stagnation. Zeus made sure Danae and his son Perseus were rescued from the sea (the unconscious). Much later in the myth, Perseus proved the oracle right. He accidentally caused his grandfather's death by wounding him with a disc he had thrown. Things locked in the unconscious will be released sooner or later, perhaps violently. The will of the Gods cannot be tampered with; new life, change, and the cyclic process must all proceed.

In the card of the Tower, the dark phallic structure rises up to meet the sky and Zeus's inseminating thunderbolt. The Tower is symbolic of the upright human body. The walled, enclosed Danae is emblematic of the Virgin Mary and the immaculate conception.[21]

The lightning flash hits the top (the head) of the Tower, symbolizing the awakening of consciousness, when in a flash, one gains insight, as some old concept of ingrained dogma is shattered. The flash is also symbolic of inspirational thought that sparks off the creative act, or a new way of thinking. The flash can create liberation, but also upheaval, if the ego is indulging in false pride, inflated ideas, narrow-mindedness, repressed rage, and artificiality. A king and queen fall from the flaming tower; it matters little who you are, or what station in life you occupy; when the lightning strikes, all must succumb.

The Tower is associated with the planet Mars. It symbolizes masculine, yang, fiery energy, our desire nature, and the impetus to forge ahead in life. There is a duality in the Martian character. The Roman god Mars, was originally a fertility god, and the father of Romulus and Remus, founders of Rome. He later became the god of battle. Mars was more civilized than his Greek counterpart Ares, a brutish warmongering god, who all other gods, except Aphrodite, despised. The positive aspect of Mars energy is reflected in the Roman god. He represents our will to achieve, our driving force, without which nothing is achieved.

Ares reflects the negative aspect of the Tower energy; violent destruction and explosive behavior which occurs when we have oppressed or negated our creativity, or when we have denied our right to stand up for our own truth.

The Tower is on the twenty-seventh path of the Kabbalistic Tree of Life, between Netzach, victory, and Hod, splendor.

This path forms the main girder of the personality, linking the creative power of Netzach and the intellect of Hod. It also links the positive and negative pillars of the Tree. This path releases energy to tear down the old structures. We have the opportunity to survey our entire personality; thus, we are forced to see what should be salvaged, thrown away, or torn down. The Hebrew letter is Peh, meaning mouth. Communication with others and within ourselves is a vital component in working on this path.

Divinatory Meaning

When the Tower appears in a spread, it indicates that those parts of ourselves we believe to be god-like will be torn down. The Tower is liberating. When we are complacent and boringly comfortable, it gives us a shake-up, which might appear frightening at first, but will lead to a necessary and positive change. The Tower energy comes suddenly and unexpectedly. You may find yourself instigating a violent outburst, saying things that have been repressed for a long time, but need expression for you to move ahead. The change can manifest in any area of your life; work, home, or relationship. If for instance, a violent outburst causes you to lose your job, perhaps it is time to look for something new which will put enthusiasm into your career. The change could release talents you never knew you had; your career could head in an entirely different direction.

Relationship issues which have been swept under the mat may come to a head now. Watch out for fireworks. If your relationship is strong, confrontation will only deepen and enhance your partnership; however, if the relationship is on shaky ground, change and breakdown may be inevitable. If your foundations are strong and deep enough, the upheaval caused by the tower energy will awaken you to the change without too much destruction. After a time, you will be thankful for the liberation and freedom you feel.

The Tower energy brings new creative and inspirational ideas. It is important to give those ideas expression, as Mars and the lightning flash are sudden and forceful. They dissipate if not snapped up and used. Any aspect of our nature, which is not truly part of our personality, will be forced out. You may find yourself asking, in what situation do I think I am better than others? Do I hide my lack of self-esteem behind a facade? Do I have the courage to accept the changes that are necessary now?

XVII THE STAR

**Key words: Faith. Optimism. Self-esteem. Hope.
Self-love. Natural talent. Life is on your side.**

Myth

Isis was the great mother of Egypt. She ruled with her
brother/husband Osiris, who was god of the Nile waters,
and the new vegetation which appeared after the flood each
year. The myth of Isis centers on the death and resurrection
of her beloved husband and her dedication to restore him to
everlasting life. When the waters of the Nile began to rise, it
was said, the goddess was mourning for her lost love, and the
tears which dropped from her eyes, swelled the river, ensuring
new life.

The seafaring Greeks of Alexandria worshiped Isis as Stella Maris, Star of the Sea. Sirius, the bright star of Isis, rising in the eastern sky, was an omen of charmed wind and calm waves.

Isis ruled the sea, the fruits of the earth and the dead. As goddess of magic, she controlled the transformation of things, beings and the elements. Isis gave hope to those who followed her. She promised, "You shall live in blessing, you shall live glorious in my protection; and when you have filled your allotted span of life and descend to the underworld, there you shall see me, as you see me now, shining."[22] The cult of Isis was later extended to the worship of the Virgin Mary, Mother of Christ.

In the card of the Star, Isis is the naked star maiden, who comes to replenish the waters of life with her tears. She is the symbol of hope eternal. Isis holds two vessels of silver and gold. The vessels contain gifts to renew the shattered dreams of humanity, after times of strife. They are the cornucopia of plenty and the magic cauldron whose bounty is always replaced. The Star's gifts are boundless; they fall like jewels upon the dry earth to restore fertility, and into the water (the unconscious) to restore our dreams. Her gifts include confidence, self-esteem, faith, hope, self-love, and self-respect. With renewed faith, the vision is possible. With confidence and self-esteem, we can once again be creative. With hope and self-love, we can fulfill the dream.

The Phoenix hovers beside Isis. It is symbolic of both the human soul and rebirth. The Phoenix is the hope which lives in each one of us, enabling us to overcome despair and experience new life after the affects of the Tower. Papyrus grass surrounds the goddess and lotus blossoms bloom in the water. The lotus is sacred to Isis and is associated with the rebirth of the god Osiris. There is more than one bloom, because we are always given more than one chance when we have failed. There is always hope for renewal. The lotus is also symbolic of the four elements; the earth, in which the plant grows, the water which supports the stalk, the air into which its perfume escapes, and the fire of the sun, from whence it draws its energy to grow.

Above the head of Isis, an eight-pointed star shines, symbolic of spiritual renewal. Seven small stars represent the seven sisters in the constellation of the Pleiades; they appear in the sky in the spring to announce the rebirth of the god and renewal of the cycle.

The Star is associated with the astrological sign Aquarius, a masculine air sign. Aquarius is symbolic of abstract thought. It is the creative idea that comes before manifestation; it is the innovator, the visionary, the creative artist. Aquarius symbolizes the highest human ideal, and in that regard describes the star maiden very well. The Star is unaware of her nakedness; she is also unaware of us as individuals, for she is totally engrossed in her task. She relates to the collective, and it is for the greater good that she bestows her gifts. Like the god Prometheus who bought fire to humanity, the Star is concerned in restoring faith, wishes and dreams to humankind.

The Star walks the twenty-eighth path, on the Kabbalistic Tree of Life, between Netzach, victory, and Yesod, foundation. This path connects the unconscious with the creative imagination. It is called the wish path, and is where tremendous creative power imbues life with hopes and dreams. There are opportunities on this path to experiment with new ideas, and inventions. The path becomes a channel of artistic, creative, and inspirational work. The Hebrew letter is Tzaddi, the fish hook, which is cast into the unconscious to see what can be brought out.

Divinatory Meaning

When the Star appears in a spread, make time to reflect, and know that everything will be all right. You have renewed trust in yourself and know that from this moment you will have the self-sufficiency to work things out. You will have another chance to begin again in some area of your life, with optimism. The Star's confidence does not come from the ego; it comes from seeing the positive side of yourself with truth and openness.

The Star offers a reprieve from difficult times; it can indicate healing after an illness, or renewed faith in oneself after a relationship breakdown. The Star, as patron of the arts, offers a renewed interest in your creative talents. You may use your skills to heal. Ask yourself these questions: What area of my life needs renewing? What do I really want in life? In what area of my life can I be the Star?

XVIII   THE MOON

**Key words: Sleep. Dreams. Past unconscious patterns.
Imagination. Fear of chaos. Illusion. Anxiety. Paranoia.**

Myth

The Triple Moon goddess has been worshiped from earliest
times. The three phases of the moon, the new, full and dark
phases, represent the three faces of the goddess.

In the new moon, crescent phase, the goddess is young and
virginal. As the moon reaches its full moon phase, the goddess
is at the height of her maturity and fertility. Finally, as the waning moon nears the end of the cycle, the dark moon phase, the
goddess ages. She becomes the wise one, the crone. This cycle is
continuing, waxing and waning, ever changing.

Females were associated with the moon as the lunar cycle of twenty-eight days coincided with a woman's menstrual cycle. A woman's seemingly magic fertility was as mysterious as the shifting face of the moon across the dark sky.

There were many different names for the goddesses associated with the moon trinity, depending on the geographical location. Although the names and myths varied, the Triple Moon goddess was worshiped as the "Great Mother" throughout the ancient world.

One such triplicity involved the goddesses Hebe, Hera, and Hecate. Hebe, the new moon phase, was the virgin, ruling the spring season and new growth. Full moon Hera was the mother, goddess of grain, harvest and the summer season. Hecate, dark moon goddess, was the crone who ruled the winter season when the earth lay dormant.

During ancient times, the night was a frightening space where wild beasts roamed. When the moon was visible, people believed the goddess was shedding light to protect them. During the dark of the moon the goddess was seen in her fearful aspect of the destroying crone. Death and the mysterious unknown were relegated to Hecate, the moon and the night.

Card number eighteen is where the Fool is challenged to enter the mysterious watery world of the moon and the realm of the feminine. He cannot proceed on his journey until he confronts his feeling nature and the mysteries of the unconscious. The moon's realm has no boundaries nor any solid structure. It is the sphere of the emotions, irrational fears and dreams. It is also the imaginary fantasy world where monsters dwell alongside heros.

In the card of the moon, Hera is holding an embryo contained within an egg. The egg represents creative potential; the embryo, the yet unformed creation, the seed for new growth. It is the gift from the unconscious.

Hera is sad; she has seen many cycles and many Fools. She knows everything that has gone before and everything that is to come. She also knows the Fool has the choice to accept the gift or take the easier path of ignorance. Will he be too afraid to step into the unknown? (Will we?)

If he does take the step, he might lose himself to the beasts of the night. He might be overwhelmed by unbridled oceanic emotions; but he has the opportunity to gain a greater depth of knowledge than before.

The wolf, companion of the goddess and guardian of the gates of the underworld (the unconscious), weeps with Hera. The wolf, long associated with the feminine, is facing extinction because of our fear of him. Symbolically, we kill off the parts of ourselves we find frightening, especially the dark Hecate side of our nature.

The moon represents past memory, including our deepest emotional responses and our changing moods. The moon card is associated with the astrological sign Pisces, which rules dreams, fantasy, illusion, and creativity. The negative aspect of Pisces is where we can get lost in the wonderful world of oceanic bliss and illusion, or succumb to the seduction of drugs or alcohol abuse. Another possibility is an addiction to helping, which is a Piscean trait.

The sign Cancer is also associated with the moon. It lives in the murky depth of the sea. Both the crab and the wolf are known as scavengers, cleaning up leftover debris (our unconscious debris).

The crab hides within its shell when it feels vulnerable, just as we close off or shut down our emotions when we feel uncomfortable. The crab walks sideways, symbolically skirting issues – a very human condition.

On the Kabbalistic Tree of Life, the Moon card is on the twenty-ninth path between Netzach – the fertile sphere of creativity, and Malkuth – the foundation of the tree where the gift from the divine manifests. The Hebrew letter for the Moon is Koph, which means the back of the head, indicating what is behind us: the past, memories, unconscious patterns.

The temptation is to ignore the call of the Moon card, but ultimately (during this cycle or the next) the Fool must embrace the unknown if he is to discover the hidden knowledge behind the High Priestess's veil. He has to confront the hidden parts of himself, the light and the dark. He must be brave enough to swim between the twin towers to enlightenment. However, the Fool cannot stay in the realm of the Moon for too long, for if he does, he may lose his way altogether. Hecate, who sits in the darkness, holds a flaming torch to guide the way to the underworld (the unconscious). She will offer safe passage back to reality only to those who dare to face the unknown parts of themselves with truth and honesty.

Divinatory Meaning

When the Moon card appears in a spread, it indicates a time to go inward. We must listen to dreams, spend time reflecting on how we feel, spend time alone, and stay with our emotions. Issues from the past may resurface. Mother or mothering issues may come to the fore. We might have psychic experiences; those who have creative abilities may be inspired. Depressed feelings or moodiness may come about without apparent reason. It is important to reflect on those feelings and moods; from where do they spring? What are their triggers?

XIX THE SUN

**Key words: The Self. Creativity. Confidence.
Self-expression. The Inner child. Optimism. Birth. Excitement.**

Myth

Eos (Aurora) was goddess of the dawn; each morning she
would rise above the horizon with outstretched wings, and
soar aloft toward the heavens. "A fresh wind was heard at her
approach," the morning star still lingered in the sky and ruddy
beams "shot the orient through with gold" and because these
beams appeared like outstretched fingers, she was called the
"rosy fingered morn."[23]

The moon and stars vanished as she advanced, but the god
Helios followed close behind. Helios is the golden orb of the
sun, which without fail rises and sets every day. He is a radiant

god, his head is surrounded with rays of light. He sets off each day in his chariot of fire, his swift horses breathing flames. Helios was the eye of the world, the celestial stickybeak; nothing escaped his notice during daylight hours.

In the card of the Sun, Eos is already heavenward bound. She heralds the dawn of the new day; she symbolizes regeneration after the dark night of the soul, reminding us that each day is a new beginning, a fresh start, filled with the promise of new life and opportunities. The unfurling of the day is symbolic of humanity's eternal optimism and innate faith in something greater.

Eos and Helios never set, they are always rising somewhere in the world, bestowing on humankind the creative energy of the sun, without which there would be no life. Helios warms and creates growth which feeds us. We revel in his sunshine, we become the divine child in his light. When the sun is shining, we are filled with joy in just being alive. Helios is the life force; when he shines down on us, we know that anything is possible.

Where Helios is the light of the sun, the sun god Apollo symbolizes the light of consciousness, of creative self-expression and clarity of thought. The sun symbolizes the prime masculine force, that creates self-awareness, and the realization of our uniqueness and individuality. In the astrological model, the sun symbolizes where we need to shine; where we, as separate personalities, find fulfillment and joy. The sun is the center of our being, it symbolizes our creativity, and the fathering principle – how we father others, and how we father ourselves. Perhaps most importantly, it symbolizes our capacity to enjoy life; to attend to the inner child, and to generate love and happiness for ourselves and others.

The myth of Phaeton, son of Helios, symbolizes what happens when we misuse the sun's energy; when we become egocentric. Phaeton doubted he was the son of Helios and asked him to prove his parentage by granting him a request. Helios agreed, but was astonished when Phaeton asked to drive the chariot of the sun for the day. Helios, bound by his honor, had to allow his son this difficult privilege. Phaeton, unacquainted with his task, soon lost control of the horses. They brought the chariot so close to earth, it scorched and burned in many places, and the rivers and seas began to boil. Zeus, alarmed, threw a thunderbolt at Phaeton, killing him instantly. The myth describes the negative aspect of the sun; if we become over-confident, vain, and arrogant, if we over-reach ourselves, we suffer burnout and cause destruction.

In the card of the Sun, the goddess Eos dwarfs the landscape; she is in full flight, with Helios close behind, his fiery horses, chomping at the bit. The landscape is still in darkness, the darkness before the dawn. The cypress trees are sacred to the gods of the underworld, our unconscious realm. The card represents our emerging unconscious energy being illuminated by the light of consciousness.

The card of the Sun walks the thirtieth path on the Kabbalistic Tree of Life, between Hod, splendour, and Yesod, foundation, the path from what is unconscious to enlightenment. The sun shines glaring light on the dark corners of our consciousness, and shows us what we have to balance. It releases things that need to see the light of the sun. This path is the highest level of human intellect, of logos and Apollo. When we are working on this path, pride and energy are released. Stamina will be tested, and it will become obvious where one lacks confidence, or the opposite, where there is too much pride. The Hebrew letter is Resh, the head, which signifies the bending of the mind to bring wisdom to the heart.

Divinatory Meaning

When the card of the Sun appears in a spread, you are filled with the life-giving force of the sun. There is joy in your life, everything will be all right no matter what drama is being enacted. The light of the sun will bring clarity to any situation. When the Sun card appears after poor health or trying times, it indicates renewal of energy and good health. For the creative artist, the Sun card symbolizes renewed confidence to explore your self expression. Creativity can express itself in many ways. Having children is, for some, the most creative act; the birth of a child may be indicated, if you are at that stage in life. This card is an expression of our inner child, and reveals the need to allow that child time to play and have fun. The Sun describes your uniqueness. Ask yourself these questions: How do I express uniqueness? How can I develop my creativity? Who am I in the world?

XX JUDGMENT

**Key words: A Calling from within. Major reassessment.
Choice. Ending karmic patterns. Change.**

Myth

The card of Judgment reawakens the sleeping hero, who is
lying in our unconscious, waiting to be called. Out of nowhere,
a divine source arouses us to continue the quest.

The hero figure is an archetype which has always existed.
The adventure of the hero usually follows a pattern; there is
a separation from the world, a penetration to some divine
source, and a life-enhancing return.[24] Myths of the hero have
been known throughout the world, from ancient times to the
present day. The content of these myths varies enormously,
but the archetype of the hero remains the same. The hero is of

humble birth and is usually conceived and born in a miraculous way. He proves his strength (physical strength or strength of character) early in life. His rise to power and recognition follows; then he has to fight the forces of evil. According to most myths, after his success, the hero commits the sin of pride (hubris), after which the hero makes the ultimate sacrifice, the giving of his life. Acceptance of his reward, immortality, follows.

The Titan hero Prometheus defied Zeus (committed hubris) by stealing fire for humanity, for which he was duly punished. Prometheus survived his ordeal and became immortal by swapping places with the suffering Centaur, Chiron. The superman, Hercules, heroically performed his twelve arduous labors, then died a martyr and ascended Mt. Olympus, where he enjoyed immortality. Psyche ventured into the underworld to procure Persephone's beauty ointment, as one of the seemingly impossible tasks set for her by the jealous Aphrodite. Psyche's quest was to regain the love of her beloved husband, Eros. Psyche committed hubris by daring to open the goddess's jar of beauty cream in order to increase her own beauty. Psyche was struck down. Eventually, she regained the love of Eros and became immortal.

In the first card of the tarot, at the beginning of the journey, the Fool was initiated into the rites of the hero. He was "called" and went forth into the world, totally unprepared, but willing. Either he had enough faith in himself and the universe to know that he would be all right, or perhaps his innocence prevented him from any preconception of the dangers the hero must face, out in the world. The card of Judgment is calling the Fool to be a hero once more. This time, though, the Fool has experienced the journey; he has met and dealt with all the archetypes along the way. He knows the meaning of fear, disruption, disappointment, loneliness, and love. The call of Judgment is far more difficult to answer; it requires a different kind of faith and trust. The Fool has experienced loss of innocence. He knows that Judgment is asking him to give more of himself.

If the Fool has completed the journey so far without too many failures, he will rise to the call to be reborn, with his life transformed and his heart full of bliss. If he is gripped by fear of the unknown, and doubts his ability to go on, he may refuse, and fall into a quagmire of self-doubt, apathy, and low self-esteem. If he ignores the call, he dies in spirit, not as the hero, but as a martyr to his ego. Our fate, like the Fool's, depends on how we respond to the Judgment card.

The call of Judgment relates to our eldership and the beginning of individuation. We have come quite far; now the time of reassessment has arrived. We look back on all the good and the bad times, the successes and failures. At this stage, we make a conscious decision either to go forward into old age with the courage of the hero, or we slip into martyrdom, where there is nothing but regret for what could have been. The hero is symbolic of that divine creature and redemptive image which is hidden in us all, only waiting to re-enter life.[25]

In the card of Judgment, an angel blows his trumpet, loud and clear. Human beings, of all ages and gender, rise to respond. The angel appears in a golden cloud, the color of the sun, symbolic of joy, happiness, and the promise of new life. The red equal-armed cross, on the angel's trumpet, symbolizes the crossroads we come to in life, and the choices we must make.

Judgment is associated with the planet Pluto, ruled by water, a feminine element. The key word for Pluto is transformation, which occurs after major life-changing events. The element water is indicative of the emotions involved. People are rising up out of the deep murky water (the deep unconscious), where old patterns are resurfacing for reassessment and liberation. Pluto breaks down things that are no longer necessary for continuing growth, and offers new life and the end to karmic patterning. The translation of the god Pluto's name appears in the Death card.

Judgment walks the thirty-first path on the Kabbalistic Tree of Life, between Hod, splendor, and Malkuth, kingdom, the path between the leader and those who follow. The first struggle toward civilization sits on this path, the foundation of the family or tribe. Walking this path means awakening to higher levels of life, a process undergone by the personality as it strives to become conscious of its inner workings. The thirty-first is a fiery path where unnecessary baggage is burned away by fire. The Hebrew letter is Shin, meaning tooth, which symbolizes the collection and retention of knowledge.

Divinatory Meaning

When the card of Judgment appears in a spread, change is inevitable. You are free to start life anew. If you have been going through a dark time, the change has arrived. Hallelujah! You will feel a sense of liberation. You may ask the question: "Why have I been resisting change for so long?" Judgment suggests that some ingrained patterning has been operating for a long time, so at first you may wonder what it is you have put out of mind.

Sometimes it is hard to recognize where changes need to be made. Old habits become a way of life. Judgment will enable you to see the broader issues, liberating you from a narrow perspective. You are being given a new lease on life. You will be full of enthusiasm and vigor. If you have been putting off making decisions, you can feel confident now to make the right one. If you have been working on a project for a long period, the time has come to reap the rewards. You have come to the end of a cycle; interesting and exciting things will follow. A relationship that has become predictable may now be seen in a different light, or you may meet a new partner. Your lifestyle may change; anything could happen to broaden your perspective. Will you hear the call to be a hero?

XXI THE WORLD

Key words: Resolution. Integration. Unity. Satisfaction. Enlightenment. Wholeness. Individuation. Success. Acknowledgment. Beyond limitation. New beginnings.

"From what the center brings
Must obviously be
That which remains in the end
And was there from eternity."

– Goethe

The World card unites all the elements of the tarot. It is difficult to grasp the complexities of the archetype, as it requires a deep philosophical knowledge of the universe. This knowledge lies somewhere in all of us. We are part of the Great Plan, and we are those complexities, by the very fact of our existence. From a psychological viewpoint, the World represents the individuated self, when all aspects of the human condition are accepted and integrated.

In the Jungian model, Self (with a capital "S") represents the whole person, mind, soul, and spirit. It symbolizes integration in its totality, light and dark, consciousness and the unconscious. With individuation, all aspects of the person are unified.

The World card symbolizes the bringing together of all opposites and the totality of the Fool's journey. He is now androgynous; his inner journey, so hard won, has reached its culmination. There is nowhere else to go now, except to begin the journey again, this time as a more mature, evolved soul. The god and goddess are united, the cycle and the wheel of life ever turning.

In the card of the World, we see the androgynous figure spinning, emulating the macrocosmic creative dance of the Lord of the Universe, Shiva, and his female counterpart, Shakti. She emulates the revolution of the planets, the dance of the atoms, and the dance of the whirling Dervish, whose spirit spirals up through the celestial heavens to unite with the divine. The figure is helped along by the four winds, Boreas, the north wind; Zephyrus, the west wind; Eurus, the east wind, and Notus, the south wind.

The dancing figure is wreathed by the Ouroboros (an ancient symbol of wholeness), the World Serpent, who wreaths the figure in an egg-shaped space, symbolically re-enacting the first act of creation. In mythology, the serpent is both male and female, and blends the forces of dark and light, yin and yang. The figure's right hand is connected to the divine source, while Yods fall from her left. Divine energy passes through her body, from the top of her head (Kether) to deep under her feet (Malkuth). This divine energy becomes the life-blood of our Mother Earth, reaching her very center. The figure is the Axis Mundi, the Axle of the World penetrating the world at its center, associated with the masculine principle; it is also the Anima Mundi, the feminine, World Soul.

In astrology, the four fixed signs (Taurus, Leo, Scorpio, Aquarius), representing solidity and permanence, are symbolic of the classical four elements thought to be the building blocks of life. These the Magician uses as his basic tools: pentacles and earth are associated with Taurus as endurance and fertility; wands and fire with Leo as courageous spirit; cups and water are associated with Scorpio, as the depth of the emotions; and Swords and air are associated with Aquarius, as intellectual clarity. The fixed signs are connected with esoteric doctrines of rebirth and spiritual development. These beliefs arise from the great concentration of energy in these signs, which have been known as gates of avatar (reincarnation of the god) and as the key symbols of the major initiations of the soul.[26]

The World card is associated with the planet Saturn, which to the alchemists represented the base metal lead, in which lay the possibility of gold. Saturn is the Lord of the material universe. Without the discipline and sense of structural reality he represents, we would achieve nothing. Saturn symbolizes the hard work we encounter on the journey to find the inner gold.

In ancient times, Saturn/Cronus and his female counterpart, Rhea were one and the same. She was the great mother goddess who gave birth to all creatures; Rhea was incorporated into classical Greek mythology by uniting her in marriage to the god Cronus. They are the personification of our wordly journey with all its cycles and phases. Both Rhea and Cronus were associated with time and the concept of the grim reaper. The scythe was synonymous with both these gods, and symbolizes the end before the beginning; it connotes the cutting down of the grain at harvest as we are cut down at death. Rhea/Cronus devoured her children, taking back in death what she had birthed.

Saturn/Rhea are linked to the limited material world. Thus, the World card reminds us of our boundaries as human beings; we cannot reach beyond human mortality. The world figure's androgynous sexuality is symbolized by a conjunction of the sun and the moon, representing the sacred marriage, the union of opposites. This uniting symbol is held within the squared circle, the alchemical symbol of wholeness.

The World walks the thirty-second and final path before the arduous climb up the Tree of Life again. This path lies between Yesod (foundation) and Malkuth (kingdom), and is the final phase of the divine manifesting in the material world. The dream has been made real, without us really understanding why. On this path we confront our individuality, and experience the beginning and the end of the cycle. The Hebrew letter is Tav, meaning the equal-armed cross, a symbol of the earth.

Divinatory Meaning

When the card of the World appears in a spread, you will have ultimate success in your endeavors. The cycle has been completed in a most satisfactory way, leaving the gate open to some new idea or venture. The World brings about happy conclusions; perhaps you have finished a project that may receive recognition, or you may have completed an educational course, or learned a new skill, that gives you a sense of pride and fulfillment. This leaves the way open to begin a new adventure. Even if a relationship is ending, it should not be too painful; perhaps the relationship has run its full course, and a new one is imminent. If you have come through a difficult time, this card indicates a resolution has been reached. The World brings with it a sense of wholeness, you get the feeling that life is good.

The World is yours for the moment: enjoy the experience, you deserve it. People will notice you and your achievements now. Sometimes the World manifests in a literal way such as travel, a new vocation, or a new home.

THE MINOR ARCANA

WHAT THE SUITS SIGNIFY

While the Major Arcana corresponds to important growth patterns and life changes on both an inner and an outer level, the Minor Arcana attends to the details of life, tells a story and describes what kind of energy is dominant in a spread.

The Minor cards are fifty-six in all: sixteen court cards and forty pip cards in four suits, corresponding to an ordinary playing deck. Wands equate with clubs, swords with spades, diamonds with pentacles, and hearts with cups. The four suits also relate to the four elements; wands to fire, swords to air, pentacles to earth and cups to water. The four tens correspond to the fifth element, ether, which is the soul latent in all things.

Interestingly, when Dr. Carl Jung, the eminent psychologist, analyzed personality, he described four basic personality functions: intuition, sensation, thinking, and feeling. According to Jung, everyone has these four functions in varying degrees. These variations are part of what make us individuals. In the tarot, the sixteen court cards have sixteen different and distinct personalities. Jung's personality functions correspond with elements and astrological groupings in the following ways:

Thinking - Swords - Air; Gemini - Libra - Aquarius

Swords' energy is revealed through the intellect; it is yang – masculine energy and corresponds to the Jungian thinking personality type. The three air signs, Gemini, Libra, and Aquarius, describe the thinking processes that run through the troubled suit of swords. The need for clear objective reasoning power, to think things through is the message of this suit. The element of air deals with abstractions; the imagination, memory, and communication of all kinds. It is not hard to understand the difficulties faced in the swords suit. The mind can play tricks when reason and logic are absent.

Intuitive - Wands - Fire; Aries - Leo - Sagittarius

Wands' energy is expressed through the element of fire. It is masculine yang energy and corresponds to the intuitive personality in the Jungian model. Three astrological signs, Aries, Leo, and Sagittarius, describe the extroverted vigor and enthusiasm of the fiery wands. They exhibit the most positive energy of all the suits, as well as the the underlying theme of optimism and the will to succeed. Fire is spirit.

Feeling - Cups - Water; Cancer - Scorpio - Pisces

The suit of cups governs emotional issues and corresponds to the element water and the astrological signs Cancer, Scorpio, and Pisces. In the Jungian model this is the feeling personality type. Cups are yin – feminine energy, and describe how we relate to and empathize with all creatures. Watery cups are a symbol of love on all levels, personal, and universal. The element of water is associated with the occult and with psychic phenomenon. Water is soul.

Sensation - Pentacles - Earth; Taurus - Virgo - Capricorn

The suit of pentacles corresponds to the element earth and the signs Taurus, Virgo, and Capricorn; the sensation personality type in the Jungian model. Earth is yin feminine energy dealing with issues concerning fertility, gestation, work, the material world, and physical or practical matters. Pentacles are where ideas (air) and the will to do (fire) become manifest. The suit of pentacles deals with how comfortable we are with ourselves on the physical plane.

When you are reading a spread, note whether there is an imbalance of suits. Many pentacles in a spread suggest issues are moving slowly and there is a need to deal with mainly practical matters. Swords emphasized in a spread indicate the need to think things through in a logical fashion and deal with matters involving negotiations, conversations, deals, gossip, statements, letters, documents, and the like. An abundance of cups points to personal, emotional, or relationship issues, while many wands suggest business, enterprise, competition, creative endeavors, and much external activity.

THE COURT CARDS

The court cards form a link between the Major Arcana and
the pip cards. They can represent actual people, or qualities
a person might be projecting. Sometimes they reflect clients'
feelings about themselves at the time of a reading. Gender is not
an issue: a woman could be using her kingly qualities; or when
a queen appears, a man might be exploring his feminine nature.

The sixteen court cards comprise four families, each with a
king, queen, knight, and princess. The kings are extroverted
and worldly in their own particular suit. The kings' energy is
masculine, confident and forthright. The queens are introverted
and receptive. That is not to say that they achieve less than the
kings. Instead, the queens are more inclined to reflect on an
issue before taking action; they allow time to digest information.

The knights represent masculine action. They lack the
thoughtfulness of the queens and the experience of the kings.
Their prime motivation is to *do*. As with all the court cards, their
mode of action varies according to the suit each represents. The
princesses symbolize the potential quality of each suit, the first
stirrings of the particular energy involved. For this reason, when
a princess card represents an actual person in a cycle, it will be a
child or someone with child-like qualities. Otherwise, the
princess cards may also signify the client's inner child, new
plans and projects, or messages that herald change.

SWORDS

Element: air
Symbols: clouds, birds, and butterflies
Color: blue

King of Swords

The king of swords uses reason and
logic when making decisions. He has
a very clever mind and is concerned
with the laws of society and the quest
for knowledge and truth. He supports
humanitarian causes. He makes a cool
lover. Although a good friend, he lacks
warmth and sensuality. This king can
represent someone who offers good
clear advice, particularly on matters
concerning the law, or medical,
philosophical, and social issues. In a
negative sense, this king can be someone who is heartless
and cruel and uses words destructively.

Queen of Swords

The queen of swords is cool, efficient,
charming, friendly, and intelligent.
She is concerned with fairness and
equality between people. When she
makes a decision, it comes from the
head, not the heart. In a relationship,
she is more a friend than a lover, and
would prefer to live alone rather than
give up her freedom. The reason for
her apparent coldness stems from her
experience of past emotional scars. The
queen of swords could appear in your
life as someone who offers friendship and advice when you
need straight answers; she will approach your questions with

diplomacy and tact. This queen may appear in your life as a woman alone, or you may have a pressing need to have more freedom and independence.

Knight of Swords

The knight of swords sweeps into your life with the force of the wind. He has an intelligent mind and can speak on a variety of subjects; in fact; he can charm you with his eloquence, only to disappear out of your life as quickly as he appeared. He can leave you feeling devastated by his disruptive influence. The knight of swords symbolizes words in action; ideas and plans start to take shape. The impetus is to act now. You feel impatient; you want movement. Some caution is needed before the signing of documents or delivering hasty words you may later regret.

Princess of Swords

The princess of swords symbolizes the stirrings of new thoughts and ideas. These can come in the form of new information to process, or abstract concepts, letters, contracts, and gossip. The princess of swords represents a quick young person with a bright mind who has plenty to say.

WANDS
Element: fire
Symbols: wands, dragon (salamander)
Colors: red, yellow, orange

King of Wands

The king of wands is a strong, friendly character. He is the successful businessman, a man of action who has the vision and ideas that lead to success. He puts his creations out into the world. He has little tolerance for fools, and he can be a little too hasty in making judgments concerning other people's behavior. The king of wands is a passionate lover who is very loyal as long as he is not restricted by a demanding partner. This king may be a person in your life, or you may have a sense of coming into your "kingly" qualities. You may be ready to put your creative endeavors out into the world.

Queen of Wands

The queen of wands holds the ouroboros (symbol of time and the continuity of life) in her hands. She is loyal, loving, and trustworthy. In love, she is passionate and exciting, but may seem overbearing to a sensitive partner. This queen speaks her mind; she is straightforward and knows what she wants from life. She is creative and generous, but needs admiration and respect from others to feel complete. This queen can represent a person with the above qualities entering your life, or you may be incorporating these qualities into your personality.

Knight of Wands

This knight represents an active, vigorous, and impatient young man. He has the vision to cure the world's ills but lacks the staying power to make it happen. He is a dashing knight, passionate and loving, who sweeps you off your feet (but only for the moment). Too rash to make sound decisions, he puts personal freedom first. The knight of wands' energy can symbolize an upsurge of energy within the self. You feel impatient; things are moving too slowly. He represents action and the will to move ahead.

Princess of Wands

The young princess and the baby dragon (or salamander) look in wonder at the new leaf sprouting on the wand. This princess can represent an energetic young person in your life or the stirrings of wands' initiative and creativity within you. This princess promises the new seed for projects and ventures.

CUPS

Element: water
Symbol: cups
Colors: blue and green

King of Cups

The king of cups is a highly intuitive, passionate man. Sometimes very secretive and withdrawn, he is not open to revealing his feelings. He excels at organizing other people's money and resources. In business, he follows hunches successfully and at times can be quite ruthless. This king hides his vulnerability, often appearing sullen. In love, the king of cups is the Heathcliff character; he is brooding, intense, and fervent, but can be possessed by feelings of jealousy and possessiveness. The king of cups is the masculine figure in your life who embodies any or all of the above attributes. He is sometimes involved in financial or secret dealings, but is also found in any of the creative fields. This king may also indicate a time when you need to explore your passionate nature or a particular time when you should not reveal your feelings.

Queen of Cups

The queen of cups is an emotional, loving woman who nurtures and cares for others around her. She is the creative artist who has a focused goal. This queen has a compassionate nature. She is easily hurt and shows her feelings openly and she is sometimes "off with the fairies," living in her own world. The queen of cups has a highly developed psychic ability and is sometimes swamped by feelings and  thoughts from uncharted places. This queen can appear in your life as the sensitive, loving person who offers a sympathetic ear and support where it is needed. She can also indicate the times when you need to nurture and be kind to yourself. This queen may also indicate psychic awareness and creativity.

Knight of Cups

Sir Galahad is the knight of cups; he belongs to the world of Arthurian legend. This romantic knight on a quest with a dream of ideal love represents creative action and imagination. He symbolizes the romantic lover who is gentle, loving, and sensitive. Music and poetry interest him. He is easily hurt and sometimes moody. The knight of cups, although he has the imagination and the dream, sometimes lacks the initiative to complete tasks. He becomes  lost in unreal schemes and has difficulty making decisions. When this knight appears in your life, he could signify a new romantic interest or creative idea. However, he could also indicate that you are about to enter a creative phase in your life.

Princess of Cups

A little mermaid is the princess of cups. The pearl in her cup symbolizes the seed of imagination and creativity, as well as the dawning of psychic ability. When the princess of cups manifests as a young person, he or she is a gentle, dreamy child who enjoys fairy tales and has a vivid imagination. On another level, that dreamy, imaginative child could correspond to your inner child, where the seed of creativity is longing to be acknowledged.

PENTACLES

Element: earth
Symbol: pentacles
Colors: red, green, and yellow

King of Pentacles

The king of pentacles is a kind, loving man. He enjoys good food and wine and is happy with his place in the world. This king is financially secure; he is a success in the business arena and has earned respect for his persistence. The king of pentacles is a reliable lover, loyal and steadfast, although at times he can be possessive and jealous.

When this king appears, you may meet a kind, generous man who is financially secure. He may be a banker or a stockbroker or work in a related field, or he could be someone who is conservative and approaches life cautiously. Some of those kingly qualities may be reflected in your life. You may feel financially secure, or may need to be more cautious in financial matters at this time.

Queen of Pentacles

The queen of pentacles is a kind, practical person who enjoys a comfortable life. Status is important to her and she will work hard to maintain appearances. She likes to be of service to the people around her and pays much attention to the details of life. In love, she is warm and sensual. In a negative sense, this queen can be selfish or too ambitious; she can also find fault with others.

The queen of pentacles may appear in your life as a person, or her queenly attributes may be just what you need in your life right now: a little luxury and a touch of comfort.

Knight of Pentacles

The knight of pentacles is a loving, steady, hard-working young man. He is ambitious and will always do a good job no matter how long it takes. As he is so thorough, he is sometimes seen as boring and slow. The knight of pentacles makes a good lover; he is sensual, tactile, and generous, even though he may lack imagination in the art of love-making. This knight is concerned with financial and material productivity. He may appear in your life as an honest, reliable person, or you may be needing some of those qualities in your life at the moment.

Princess of Pentacles

Daffodils and blossoms symbolize the spring season and potential new growth represented by the princess of pentacles. She suggests the need to make an idea or plan material, to bring it down to earth. This can manifest as either a new study, apprenticeship, or ideas for material and financial improvements. The princess of pentacles can represent a young, robust person who is steadfast and loyal; or, your inner child may feel a sense of well-being and groundedness.

THE MINOR ARCANA CARDS IN DETAIL

The forty Minor cards come under the umbrella of the first ten numbered Major cards, from the Magician to the Wheel of Fortune. In addition, on the Kabbalistic Tree of Life, the Minor cards are designated to the ten spheres (sephiroth). All life springs from Kether, moves down the Tree, and becomes manifest in Malkuth.

THE TENS

The four tens correspond to the Wheel of Fortune. Fate and destiny are inherent factors here; the tens represent the culmination of each suit and its element. The aces at the beginning of the cycle symbolize the pure energy of the suit; the tens, at the end of the cycle, symbolize the full experience. We have moved down to Malkuth on the Tree of Life, where the four tens in their respective suits become manifest and complete the cycle. The four princesses also reside here, symbolizing birth of the seed.

Ten of Swords

The card depicts a figure in a desperate bid to reach distant shores. Swords are piercing his body from all angles. The injuries to the figure are grossly exaggerated; however, sometimes a bad back is indicated by this card. Metaphorically speaking, you could be stabbed in the back by gossip and slander. Swords symbolize the power of words. The hurt usually comes from words spoken and foretells the end of a cycle of arguments and disputes. The message in this card may be that you leave a bad situation to go to a better and brighter future. A holiday could relieve tension and mental stress, or help could come from far away.

Ten of Wands

The ten wands on the woman's back represent all her resources, skills, and ambitions. She is bending low with the load; her road is rough and a brick wall stops her progress. When this card appears in a spread, it suggests you are taking on too much responsibility and worry. This can manifest in physical exertion, or taking too much responsibility in a relationship, or in business and career matters. Although this card foretells success, the lesson is to delegate some of your responsibilities to others. Sometimes this card indicates being the martyr or using your burdens as an excuse to avoid breaking away from a bad situation.

Ten of Cups

In the ace of cups, a fairy has only just discovered the magic pot; in the ten she is sharing love, joy, and happiness with us all. When you receive the gift of the ten of cups in a reading, you will experience fulfillment on all levels. Your dreams will come true, especially on a personal, emotional level. The message of this card is that when you feel happy and full of love, others around you will also benefit.

Ten of Pentacles

Central to this card is the family; not only the immediate family, but the traditional and cultural heritage that forms the family of humans today. It is the richness of the family, not just in monetary terms, but in our memories, histories, and myths that stands behind us when we draw this card in a spread. You will find answers to questions if you look to the elders and wise ones from the past. On another level, the ten of pentacles suggests financial security, family celebrations, family support, or the burdens that only family can impose.

THE NINES

Number nine means completion and corresponds to the Hermit. The nines describe the end of the journey; we act alone, with inner conviction. The four nines reside in Yesod, the unconscious mind, the stuff that dreams are made of.

Nine of Swords

A woman wakes in the night gripped by fear. She feels depressed and does not know which way to turn. Life is at an all-time low, and there seems no solution to her problems. Sometimes this card appears when there have been real difficulties to overcome that only time and the universe can heal. However, sword energy deals with the thinking processes. Things may not be as bad as they seem. In the light of day, a clear head will find solutions in many situations. Sometimes the answers lie in self-knowledge and inner wisdom.

Nine of Wands

This man is very defensive. He has positioned himself protectively in front of his eight wands, which represent his resources or his problems. He is used to opposition and has had to fight many times to protect his vulnerability. He clutches his last wand, symbolizing the one last move he has to make. He needs confidence to put that last wand in place along with the others. When you draw the nine of wands, your opinions and convictions may be questioned. You may need the light of the Hermit to walk your own path. This card may appear when you have been through a lengthy dispute, trial or situation where you feel you have had enough. You have given this issue as much as you can; now you are being asked to try one more time. The irrepressible energy of the wands will take up the challenge.

Nine of Cups

The nine of cups is known as the wish card; things could not be better. You are emotionally, physically and mentally content with the world. In fact, you are on "cloud nine." This card indicates fulfillment and contentment in all areas of life.

Nine of Pentacles

The nine of pentacles depicts a well-dressed woman leisurely enjoying her garden alone. It is a fine day; butterflies, symbolizing freedom, flutter about her. The nine of pentacles augurs success, self-sufficiency, and inner and outer wealth. You may have had to wait a long time for this moment, and you have done it with little help. You have made it, even though it is a little lonely at times. Now you can sit back and enjoy the fruits of your labor.

THE EIGHTS

The four eights correspond to Strength. In the eights, we meet the challenges of life with courage, creativity, and confidence. On the Tree of Life, the four eights reside in Hod, which represents the intellect and the concrete mind.

Eight of Swords

The image in this card is a blindfolded woman. She is bound and fenced in by eight swords and her feet are stuck in the mud. Look closely; her bonds are not tied; she could easily release herself and walk away. She needs the courage of Strength to face her reality. It is only her fear that is keeping her bound and in an oppressed condition. This is a sword card, so the oppression is a mental one. The woman feels the encouraging warmth of the sun. She will use her mind creatively to get out of this situation. However, the choice is hers, and she may prefer to stay in bondage rather than face reality.

Eight of Wands

The eight of wands combines the speed of air, the courage of fire, and eventually, when the wands come to ground, the groundedness of earth. Speed, action, and movement are indicated in the eight of wands. Life will be speeding up and new activities, letters, or engagements may enter your life now. Sometimes travel is imminent, either physically or mentally.

Eight of Cups

The image on the card is that of the goddess Persephone returning to her underworld home for the winter cycle. The myth describes how we go through life quite happily, taking for granted our seven cups. Then something happens; a broken relationship, the loss of a loved one, or even the realization that those seven cups can no longer fulfill the dream. At this, we go into our private underworld alone, questing for our eighth cup. This takes us on a lonely and painful trip; but with inner strength, we come back in the spring renewed. On another level, we may go on a physical trip, hoping to feel renewed and fulfilled.

Eight of Pentacles

A highly skilled and successful smith is working at his craft. This card indicates profitable times ahead when you can use your skills to your advantage. The eight of pentacles is usually connected to money and career matters; however, its meaning can be applied to any area of life where you need to be skillful. Sometimes this card comes up when a person has "too many fingers in too many pies" and there is a need to focus talent. The card could also be suggesting that it's time to take your skills out into the wider world.

THE SEVENS

The four sevens correspond to the Chariot. The sevens require concentrated effort to achieve success; the goal is to move ahead despite adversity. The sevens dwell in Netzach, the sphere of creativity.

Seven of Swords

The airy seven of swords is about mind games. The figure in the card is trying to run away with all seven swords but cannot quite make it. He is cunning as a fox and changeable as the shifting sands on the beach. When you draw this card, think carefully. Sometimes the seven of swords indicates schemes that do not work or that need to be modified in some way. You or someone else may be planning a surprise, so a little cunning may be necessary to cover your tracks. Acts of daring, impulsive acts, and under-cover acts as well as detective work all come with this card. The figure in the card is acting alone; he is trying to hide his intentions from the people on the hill. This card indicates you may need to keep your ideas and plans to yourself and use caution when discussing important intentions. Another possibility with the seven of swords is that you will try to avoid or manipulate the truth; however, tact and diplomacy will sometimes save a situation.

Seven of Wands

In the card, a farmer has successfully grown a crop of wheat. He has put in the effort and is about to reap the harvest; he has fought off his adversaries who lay claim to his hard-earned crop. Despite the problems he has faced, he is on top of things. There is plenty of energy to fight for one's rights with the fiery wands, which is what you might have to do when this card appears. Make a stand when challenged; know your rights. Sometimes the seven of wands indicates you are contending with difficulties very well and no one can take advantage of you.

Seven of Cups

In the card, a woman stands in the rain and mist obscures her vision. She cannot see the seven cups clearly, nor their contents. The woman is perplexed. She knows she must make a choice but is too confused to make a decision; she must wait for the rain to stop and the mist to clear. When you draw this card, it suggests you are at a crossroad and must make a choice, usually an emotional one. You cannot make up your mind which cup to take, for they all seem desirable but you can have only one. Give yourself time before making a decision.

Seven of Pentacles

A woman has planted her seven seeds in the ground. She feels confident they will sprout because she knows from past experience and other harvests that good care and patience will bring results. When the seven of pentacles is in a spread, it suggests gestation. If you are setting up a business, planning a new career or concentrating on any area of life that will ultimately bear fruit, so long as you have prepared your ground well, you will eventually reap the rewards. Concentrated effort and patience will bring profits.

THE SIXES

The four sixes correspond to the card of the Lovers. Six is a number of harmony and balance; these cards signify the opportunity to find equilibrium by making the right choices in life. According to the Kabbalah, the four sixes dwell in Tiphareth, where harmony is reached. The knights also dwell here; they represent the masculine force of each suit coming together.

Six of Swords

This card describes finding peace after a troubled time. No matter how difficult a situation, there is always light on a distant shore and a guardian angel to guide you there. The six of swords gives respite after illness, or any other event in your life where there has been mental pressure and stress. Life is improving and you are entering a more peaceful phase. This card could indicate a move of some kind that will ultimately improve your life.

Six of Wands

Both the jockey and his horse are the winners in this card. Much training and hard work, along with the wands' impetus to win, have brought them both to this victorious culmination of effort. When this card appears in a spread, victory is sweet. You are about to receive the rewards for the choices you have made and all your hard work. The six of wands usually suggests success in business, career and creative enterprises, but can also foretell victory in any personal endeavor.

Six of Cups

The six of cups is connected to past memories. Sometimes we are filled with nostalgia for the good old days. Some of us are so rooted in the past that it stops our progress because not all our past experiences were rosy. When the six of cups appears, someone, a past lover, friend or foe, may reappear in your life, giving you an opportunity to renew an old acquaintance or perhaps work through an old emotional issue. The Major Arcana card corresponding to the six of cups, the Lovers, depicts a triangle between the Lovers and the angel. A triangle is also suggested in the six of cups; a third person from the past could become involved in an emotional situation with you.

Six of Pentacles

The six of pentacles denotes equality between all people, giving and receiving with no strings attached. You may receive gifts of material value or simply gifts of love. You may be the donor, able to give with an open heart. Practical help may come when you need it. With this card you are not on your own; there are others who are willing to share with you, and you with them. There is a karmic message in the six of pentacles: you reap what you sow.

THE FIVES

All the fives contain some form of conflict. The fives correspond to the Hierophant, so the conflict is the struggle to be "true to oneself" in the face of adversity. The four fives reside in Geburah, the sphere of unmitigated truth on the Tree of Life.

Five of Swords

The five of swords depicts a no-win situation. In the card, even though one man has taken charge of the raft, leaving the other two to fend for themselves, he still has to face the vast ocean. Swords symbolize the mind and communication; the standing man is not open to negotiation. With this card, you may find yourself in a situation where you need to choose your words carefully and be open to negotiation over an important issue. You might think you have the upper hand and turn away, but then find this is not the final outcome. Carefully chosen words can give you power, especially if they come from your inner voice. You may find that someone has the upper hand over you. Accepting defeat is difficult but sometimes it is necessary if we are to move on.

Five of Wands

The five of wands depicts the competitive spirit of the wands' energy. In the card, five men put on a mock display of aggression. four of them stand together in a variety of threatening poses against one man. With this card, challenges may arise requiring you to defend yourself. This is usually in a business situation and may be stimulating, since it gets the adrenaline running. Your options may be questioned, and you may have to prove your point over an issue. The fives are action-packed. You may have to compete in either worldly or emotional affairs.

Five of Cups

The five of cups denotes an emotional loss of some kind. The woman in the card is riding the waves on a sea of emotion. The three spilled cups are irretrievable. She feels distraught and cannot see any hope for the future. At the moment the woman is so lost she is unaware of the two remaining cups and the fertile life that is being offered to her. All is not lost when you draw this card; you may have to let go of an emotional issue to find the other cups in your life. They could hold something of greater value than what you have lost. It is a time of pain and melancholy, but fortunately this state is only temporary.

Five of Pentacles

The five of pentacles depicts a woman and child out in the snow on a cold, dark night. Feeling miserable, she looks through the window and sees a group of people who are warm and enjoying themselves. The woman has just stepped over two pentacles without noticing. The child at her side symbolizes her creativity. This card sometimes deals with real poverty in the material world. More often than not, however, the five of pentacles suggests a poverty of mind and spirit where self-esteem and worth are at an all-time low. There is still hope in this situation, because the fives bring change; the feeling of deprivation is temporary.

THE FOURS

The fours correspond to the Emperor. He stands for stability, authority, and discipline. Four is the most stable number, signifying reason and logic. Chesed is the first concept of organization on the Kabbalistic Tree; this is where the four fours reside.

Four of Swords

A woman has turned her back on her world. She has been asleep for some time; the candle has burnt out and the door is bolted. The red poppies on her bedspread are associated with deep sleep and the unconscious; the Emperor is taking a break. The message of this card is the need to temporarily retreat from the world to recuperate after a difficult time, or to allow time to become reconciled with an issue. Swords represent our thinking patterns.

This card calls for time to think things through quietly and thoroughly. The sun shining through the window promises solutions.

Four of Wands

In the four of wands we see yet another celebration; it is a time of prosperity and movement to a more stable period of life, symbolized by the marriage couple. They have gained the freedom to forge ahead in their new life, but to achieve this they have to leave their old life, childhood, and family behind. This card augurs well for the future and could incorporate a change of residence or changes for the better in the domestic environment.

Four of Cups

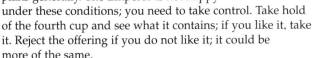

A woman sits in her garden. She has been emotionally fulfilled but is now bored and dissatisfied with her life; she is uninterested in the three cups before her and is dreaming of greener pastures. A fourth cup, of which she is unaware, hovers behind her. Sometimes this card reflects a disappointing or hurtful relationship, or a relationship that has lost its romance. This feeling of depression and boredom could apply to other areas of life such as career or thwarted plans generally. The Emperor is not happy under these conditions; you need to take control. Take hold of the fourth cup and see what it contains; if you like it, take it. Reject the offering if you do not like it; it could be more of the same.

Four of Pentacles

Traditionally this is the card of the miser. The Emperor is immobilized; his wealth has become his prison. He sits rigidly in his black and white world. This card warns about becoming obsessed by material gain and self-importance; it also warns against worrying about not having enough. There is financial security when you draw this card. You can relax and enjoy life. The man holds on to what he considers is important. This need not signify his material possessions; it could be his pride, his self-esteem, self-worth, or even his privacy. With this card, setting up boundaries is important. Protect yourself from the demands of others who ask too much of you.

THE THREES

The four threes symbolize creative fertility in their own particular element and correspond to the Empress, the great mother goddess. All the threes hold her productivity and abundance within their interpretation. On the Tree of Life, the four threes dwell in Binah, the first hint of form. The four queens are also represented here as the prime feminine force.

Three of Swords

The traditional keyword for this card is sorrow. A woman stands in the rain on a dark night, holding a red rose over her heart. A figure, illuminated by the lamplight, hurries out of her life. The three of swords symbolizes a great sorrow; it is usually rooted in the past and not yet resolved. The red rose is symbolic of love; her sorrow has a strong emotional background. When the three of swords appears in a spread, it is time to grieve and allow the rain to wash away the tears of yesterday. The rain is cleansing and offers renewal. The three of swords is a creative card in that it symbolizes a release of painful memories.

Three of Wands

The fiery nature of wands has taken the vision of the two and developed it to produce success and achievement in the three. In the card, a woman stands looking out to sea. She has an aura of success about her; she can now afford to stand by to watch her ships carry on the business of the day with confidence.

The three of wands indicates good results in any business venture. There are opportunities to expand and sometimes offers come from overseas or you may travel to further your career. The general feeling is one of growth and expansion, not only in business but in all spheres of life.

Three of Cups

The three of cups symbolizes celebration after the harvest; enjoy yourself now as it is autumn and there will be plenty of preparation to be done before the cycle begins again. Three dancing women are enjoying the Empress's bounty. This card is feminine in nature and can appear to announce the birth of something; an idea, a creative project, or a child. Above all, the card heralds good times; there will be joy, friendship, and celebration.

Three of Pentacles

The three of pentacles represents recognition and praise for skills. A prima ballerina is receiving acknowledgment for her achievement. She has had to work hard to reach the top of her profession and now is reaping the reward for her efforts. Sincere effort does not go unrewarded. When the three of pentacles appears you will receive your dues. Success is yours in return for persistent and dedicated labor; this may come in the form of money, a prize or an award.

THE TWOS

The twos represent duality, masculine and feminine, light and dark, yin and yang. The four twos correspond to the High Priestess; she brings together opposing forces. In Kabbalistic terms, the four twos dwell in Chokmah, the dynamic power-house of the universe; the first projection of an idea. The four kings are also represented as the prime masculine force.

Two of Swords

The two of swords is depicted by a vulnerable young girl walking a tight-rope over a rough sea, holding two crossed swords over her heart. She is trying to balance opposing forces within herself and is caught up in so much emotional turmoil that she is afraid to remove the blindfold in case she topples into the sea. This is the card of stalemate when a clear head is needed to clarify a situation that is emotionally charged. This card often appears when there is an issue involving negotiations or conflicts between partners. Trying to be fair on all sides can create a state of tension or inertia. By facing the facts, tension will be broken and the situation will be resolved.

Two of Wands

The two of wands is symbolized by a businessman. He is already successful, but the fiery nature of wands still lures him to future visions and expansion. A partnership may be indicated by this card, one that may take you beyond your present level of success; or you may feel bored with your achievements and want to expand your horizons in some other way. There is success with this card, but it is often accompanied by a sense of restlessness. New plans and deals are suggested; perhaps you need to travel to expand the vision.

Two of Cups

The two of cups depicts a balanced and harmonious relationship between two people. Sometimes the card suggests a new romantic relationship or a renewal of an existing one. Often this card indicates other relationships, such as business partnerships or someone offering platonic friendship. The relationship indicated by the two of cups is one of equality when two people meet with acceptance. In some situations, the two of cups simply means feeling balanced within the self.

Two of Pentacles

The two of pentacles symbolizes balancing
the ups and downs of life; it suggests these
ups and downs are not of a serious nature.
Moderation is the key word with this card.
If you are working too hard, rest is required.
If you are putting too much energy into a
relationship, look to your needs. If you
overspend, the debt will still have to be
paid. Mood swings, money fluctuations,
and being unable to make up your mind
come with this card. You may need to get
your priorities right to solve a dilemma. Generally, the
two of pentacles means balancing factors in your life.

THE ACES

The four aces are the tools of the Magician. The aces of swords
(air), wands (fire), pentacles (earth), and cups (water) represent
pure energy in their elements. On the Kabbalistic Tree, the four
aces dwell in Kether, the crown, the point where life wells up
from the great manifest, the godhead.

Ace of Swords

The ace of swords represents intellectual
energy. In the card, the upright sword cuts
through all that is unnecessary to get to the
crux of the matter; the eyes of truth are ever
watchful. This card symbolizes fresh ways of
thinking and indicates the need for an
approach coming from logic and reason
where the head rules the heart. Thoughts can
become clear and uncluttered. The upright
sword cuts both ways; it can indicate tri-
umph and success, but it also cuts away
outworn mental attitudes. Sometimes this process seems
destructive, but it is necessary.

Ace of Wands

A hand appears from sun-drenched clouds; divine energy is directed at a lone wand and small shoots respond and grow. The fiery ace represents a powerful surge of creative, intuitive energy. It is the spark needed to begin new projects, the drive to make dreams a reality. The ace of wands indicates new life, new business ventures, new ideas that expand your horizons. Above all, this ace is full of optimism and looks to the future.

Ace of Cups

In this card a forest fairy discovers the Well of Happiness, known in myth as the Grail, the fountain of youth, and the Cornucopia of plenty. The earthenware pot reminds us of our mortality while the fountain represents divine love. An ancient spiral design symbolizes the continuum of the life/death cycle. The ace of cups is the energy of love and the emotions. When this card appears in a spread, it suggests a new relationship, a feeling of emotional contentment or of gaining your heart's desire. This includes any new situation that comes from the heart and not the head.

Ace of Pentacles

The ace of pentacles is represented in the Spiral Tarot by the World Tree. Earth Mother goddess reaches out to the heavens. Her branches are laden with life while her feet are rooted in the ground. The ace of pentacles symbolizes new life on the material plane. It can herald success and prosperity, financial gain, a new career or business or a new sense of self-worth and status. Life is stable; a sense of well-being comes with this card.

READINGS

YOU AND YOUR CLIENTS

Reading the tarot should be a two-way experience. The better the rapport between reader and client, the more information is revealed. Some readers are exceptionally psychic and do not want or need their clients to pose questions or offer information about their lives. Other readers would prefer the client to ask the tarot a particular question. Some clients test the reader and will not reveal anything about themselves or the reason for their presence. Unless the reader is a psychic, such a client will not get the best results and the reading will be rather mechanical.

One of the greatest difficulties during a reading is the client who expects the tarot to reveal the future in a very predictive way. Relationship issues often cause very pressing questions to be asked. "When is my lover going to appear?" If the client's self-esteem is low, (this is usually revealed in a reading), then the image projected by the person is not conducive to attracting a partner. The tarot encourages self-knowledge. During a reading, ways of overcoming feelings of inadequacy and fear of failure are often revealed. The ability to discuss these kinds of issues with a client is more helpful than a predictive formula.

When a client feels good about him or herself, the lover is usually around the next corner, or the contract or career move the client wants is about to be offered.

BEGINNING A READING

Before starting any reading, the cards should be well-shuffled. Some readers prefer to shuffle first. The client repeats this process, then cuts the cards into three separate decks and re-assembles them into one deck. The reader then takes the cards off the top. Other readers shuffle the cards, then spread them out for the client to choose the required number. There are no fixed rules.

SIGNIFICATORS

Some readers choose a card they feel reflects the client.
This is usually, but not always, a court card. Sometimes the
significator is chosen using the astrological model, like a court
card corresponding to the client's birthday. At other times the
reader chooses a court card to reflect the present mood of the
client, or if the question concerns a new relationship, the knight
of cups is a favorite. Other readers use the first card drawn to
see what is significant in the client's life at present.

SPREADS

There are many different spreads you can use; after a while you may even want to design one for yourself. It is usually necessary to use two or three spreads during a reading to get to the heart of the matter.

Included here are the Spiral Spread and three of my other favorite layouts: the Three Card Spread, the Star and the traditional Celtic Cross. The Three Card Spread gives an immediate feel for the energy around the client. The Star Spread looks at the life of the client on a more profound level. The Celtic Cross is a good inclusive spread that describes what is going on in a client's outer world.

THE THREE CARD SPREAD

The Three Card Spread is good for beginners because too many cards can initially be confusing. However, it is also a useful tool for the experienced reader, as its meaning is usually immediate.

Cards 1, 2, and 3 can be read as past, present, and future or self, relationship, and other, or:

Card 1.   What kind of situation is manifest now.

Card 2.   What influences the situation.

Card 3.   How the situation may develop.

Three Card Spread - Sample Reading

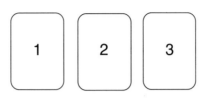

A young, self-employed man is having difficulties getting a government building contract which would give him work for the next six months. There is plenty of competition (five of wands) but he remains optimistic. The Emperor in the position of "what influences the situation" represents the government body. The third card, six of wands, indicates that he may win the contract since victory and success come with this card.

Sometimes the third card may not give sufficient information. For example, if the three of swords turned up in position three, one could assume that something from the past could be blocking the young man's success. In this case, another card could be drawn to clarify matters.

THE SPIRAL SPREAD

The Spiral Spread has been devised for the reader to use with the Spiral Tarot deck. The reading uses ten cards selected from the full deck, since ten cards constitute a cycle.

We constantly attempt to complete cycles; new projects, relationships and other life situations have a beginning, run their course, and come to a conclusion or resolution.

Although the spread is primarily about self-examination, it was designed to be used for any sort of cycle. Knowing who we are and what we need augurs well for good relationships and successful ventures.

Card 1. The self: where you are now on your journey.

Card 2. An influence that is operating now: what is significant about this reading.

Card 3. Things that are unconscious about the self: past, forgotten memories.

Card 4. What you are already conscious of, or becoming aware of.

Card 5. What you need for fulfillment.

Card 6. What you think you need, or expect to happen in the situation.

Card 7. Help along the way; this could be a person, or positive attributes of the self.

Card 8. What hinders you and makes life difficult: what the self refuses to acknowledge.

Card 9. Where the situation is leading and how you will deal with it.

Card 10. The outcome.

If, at the end of the reading, any cards seem ambiguous, fan the whole pack face down and have the person choose three more cards to clarify the card in question. For example:

The Devil card is drawn in position 5. (What you need to find fulfillment.) The Devil always indicates fear, bondage, or limitations in our lives. If you are not already clear about precisely what this card in this position signifies, a Three Card Spread should reveal what is blocking fulfillment in this particular case.

Spiral Spread - Sample Reading

Nella came to me with a difficult family problem. She has four children, two sons from a first marriage and two daughters from her successful second marriage. The family unit has worked very well in every respect but one: the boys have always fought with one another.

Nella, who has been responsible for all decisions concerning her sons since their father is unresponsive, feels that deep-seated paternal issues are the cause of their mutual hostility.

At a time when the two young men were in their twenties, their constant bickering had culminated in a stand-off where there was no communication between them at all. Nella felt that she was being torn apart by their bitterness. On the morning of the reading, Nella's sons had actually spoken to each other for the first time in months.

Spiral Spread-Sample Reading for Nella

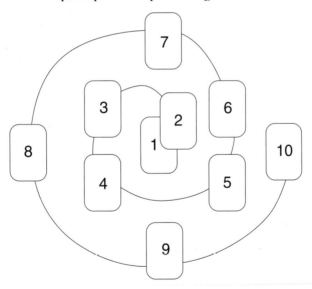

Card 1. Princess of Cups

Nella was delighted that her sons had responded to each other. At this stage, the Princess of Cups' offering was tentative.

Card 2. Queen of Wands

I saw the image on this card as a reflection of Nella herself; generous and kind, loyal to both her sons. It was also possible that this was how her sons saw her. Despite the difficulties, Nella had been able to maintain her position in the family with dignity.

Card 3. Seven of Pentacles

Nella was doing what most parents do when their children have problems: she was blaming herself, wondering what she had done wrong. The seven of pentacles here reminded Nella that in the past she did sow her seeds well in the way she raised her sons. This seven is a card of gestation; impatience will not bring good results. The suggestion was that Nella must allow the cycle to resolve itself.

Card 4. Two of Pentacles

Nella was very conscious of maintaining balance in the family dynamic from one day to the next. In a very visual sense, the two of pentacles describes Nella holding her sons' problems in either hand while she maintained the balance.

Card 5. The Moon

This was the first major card in the reading. The Moon reaches into the unconscious depths of the mind. Perhaps the situation had triggered some sad memories for Nella. The problems her sons presented may have been be a repeat of something in her own past that she needed to reflect upon. The Moon card carries illusion and confusion in its complex message. Perhaps Nella needed to let go of the illusory happy family. I suggested to Nella that the time was right to encourage her sons to become more independent. This would mean it was also a time for Nella to grieve over this change, then look to her personal endeavors for fulfillment.

Card 6. Ace of Pentacles

Nella quite reasonably expected a fresh start for her family life; the ace of pentacles is full of promise for the future.

Card 7. Nine of Wands

I had the feeling the figure in this card represented Nella's attitude in the cycle. It looked as if she would have to remain strong, as there seemed to be another hurdle to cross. Nella would find the inner strength to cope with whatever presented.

Card 8. The Empress

The Empress appeared as the second Major card in the Spiral. Importantly, both the Moon and the Empress denote mothering issues. Nella wanted to remain the bountiful loving mother. She could do so, but what hindered her in this cycle was her refusal to let go of her creations, her sons.

Card 9. Strength

Strength is the third Major in the reading. The card suggested that Nella would deal successfully with the situation, not by forceful means, but with confidence and love. The message of the Strength card is reinforced by the nine of wands in position seven, which suggested help would be available in the cycle. Throughout this reading, Nella was the key figure. It seemed to be more to do with her than with her sons' situation.

Card 10. The Tower

The cycle must come to an end; change is inevitable. The Tower energy will sweep away the old family formula. Nella's sons were no longer children. The Tower in this position suggested to me that Nella's sons would soon leave home to make their own way.

Elaboration of Nella's Spiral Reading

Nella felt that the eighth card, the Empress, needed further explanation. We fanned the remainder of the pack and Nella chose three cards to clarify the message of the Empress:

Card 1. Two of Wands

My intuitive feeling was that the figure in the two of wands represented Nella's younger son. He had developed his skills sufficiently at this point to feel cramped and frustrated by his situation. He needed to move out of his small world and into the larger community, where he could seek to fulfill his ambitions.

Card 2. Four of Swords

The central card is the four of swords; I felt that the sleeping woman in the card was Nella. It seemed she needed to take a back seat and allow her sons to explore their futures, each in his own way. The Empress is repeating her message: Let them go.

Card 3. Three of Wands

The figure in the third card described an attribute of Nella's older son. This man is more in touch with the intuitive feminine side of his nature. (It is quite appropriate that the female figure in card three expresses this aspect in a male.) Nella told me that this son wants to travel. It seemed he might do so; at least the card suggests that fulfillment lies out there, not in the confines of the family home.

The Tower in the outcome position looked so violent that Nella drew three more cards to clarify it:

Card 1. Queen of Cups

Like the queen of cups, Nella is a loving and sensitive woman. If we look closely at The queen of cups, we see she is very focused on the cup in her hand. She sees nothing else. I felt this card represented Nella's inability to see beyond her present emotional state.

Card 2. Ten of Cups

The ten of cups promises that the changes the Tower brings will ultimately benefit the family unit. The sons' leaving will not lessen the love felt between family members; in fact, separation might enable the young men to see each other with the love and respect that lies beneath their hostility.

Card 3. Knight of Wands

It seemed to me that the energy held in the knight of wands was about to make itself felt. The resolution of this cycle is imminent. The knight of wands is impatient. He wants action now!

THE STAR SPREAD

The six-pointed Star (hexagram) is symbolic of the union of the god and the goddess. Only the Major cards should be used in this spread.

The Star Spread is designed for an in-depth look at the inner world of the client which, in turn, is reflected in the outer world. This spread should not be repeated constantly in the hope that the cards drawn will suit the vanity of the client.

The cards in this spread ask the following questions of the client:

Card 1. What is most important to my inner world now?

Card 2. What gives me strength and fortitude?

Card 3. Who guides me?

Card 4. What or who protects me?

Card 5. What is missing in my life?

Card 6. What do I need to learn?

Star Spread - Sample Reading

A woman who is a creative writer came to me, confused and worried about the changes in her life. This woman, whom we shall call Joan, works alone and enjoys the solitude and peace of her small world. Now that her work has been noticed by the public, she finds herself uncomfortably plunged into the business world of contracts, meetings, letters, and like commitments. This was her reading:

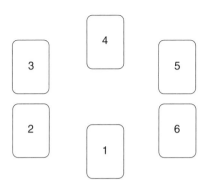

Card 1. The Hierophant

What is most important to Joan now is to remain true to herself and still function effectively in society. She finds she is getting advice from many people. She must listen, but still follow her inner voice.

Card 2. Death

What gives her strength and fortitude? The ability to accept the death of her old life is her strength. This is not to say all aspects of her life must change; Joan has always been a shy and retiring woman who has avoided using her masculine energy to promote herself. It seems that is about to change.

Card 3. The Wheel of Fortune

Who guides her? The wheel of fate and destiny does. Things are out of her hands now and she must accept her fate and trust in the universe. Joan has worked hard in her chosen career. Life is about to reward her efforts. She has nothing to fear.

Card 4. The Chariot

What protects her? She is protected by the objectivity of the Chariot. The aim here is to move forward in life, controlling her emotions in order to be victorious. The charioteer is the solar hero who goes out to conquer the world; again, an indication it is time for Joan to use her inner masculine.

Card 5. The Tower

What is missing in her life? The excitement of changes?
Joan must give way to the power of the Tower and be prepared
to accept new ideas rather than adhering to the old comfortable
ways. Many things will probably change for Joan now that her
success is recognized. It is most important that she accepts the
changes while retaining her sense of self, not succumbing
to grandiosity.

Card 6. Temperance

Joan needs to learn to balance her inner and outer worlds.
From now on, it seems she may not return exclusively to her
hermit-like existence, but develop acceptance of her role in
society. With the cards of the Wheel of Fortune, Death, and the
Tower in the spread, change is inevitable. If she heeds the advice
of Temperance and creates a harmonious balance, she can have
the best of both worlds.

THE CELTIC CROSS SPREAD

The Celtic Cross spread is an all-time favorite. Shuffle the full
deck, and lay the cards out as follows:

Card 1.   The Significator, or what is significant in the person's
life now.

Card 2.   The present influence surrounding the client's
question.

Card 3.   What is helping or hindering the situation.

Card 4.   The basis of the situation; how past experience is
influencing the present question.

Card 5.   What has been resolved; the recent past, or an
influence that has recently lost importance.

Card 6.   What the client can learn from this situation; the
possible future outcome.

Card 7.   The immediate future. What will happen next
regarding the question.

Card 8. The way the client sees herself in this present situation.

Card 9. How others are contributing to the situation; influences over which the client has no control.

Card 10. Hopes and fears. A positive card shows the person's hopes; a negative card shows his or her fears.

Card 11. The probable outcome.

Card 12. Helps to clarify the outcome.

Card 13. Helps to clarify the outcome.

Celtic Cross Spread - Sample Reading

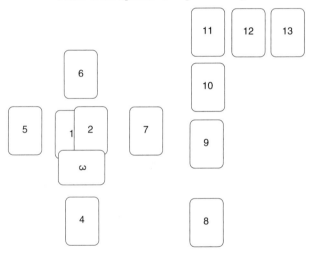

A young woman, whom I shall name Marcia, came to me with a question concerning a relationship. She had been in a bad relationship for quite some time and was trying to pluck up enough courage to do something about it. This kind of question is difficult for the reader. The client must take responsibility for her own decisions, but it is up to the reader to offer encouragement and support. Cards 1, 2 and 3 described her situation perfectly. Those three cards alone seemed to make it obvious where Marcia was heading.

Card 1. Eight of Swords

Here is Marcia; she feels bound and restricted, but it is only her fear that keeps her in that position. Marcia has been in the relationship for a number of years. Even though she is unhappy, life is predictable and the thought of being on her own is daunting.

Card 2. Eight of Cups

This card indicates that Marcia feels unfulfilled emotionally and needs to go on an inner journey to find what is truly in her heart. This would be a big step for Marcia, as she would have to make that journey alone.

Card 3. Seven of Cups

The seven of cups describes Marcia's confusion. At this time she cannot see her way out of the difficult situation. The card indicates Marcia has many choices ahead, although at the moment she cannot see beyond her present pain. This card warns about being too hasty. Marcia needs to give herself some time. Then, when the mists clear, she will make the right decision.

Card 4. Four of Pentacles

This card in this position, signifying what has been learned from past experience, suggests that Marcia has learned to protect her vulnerability by putting up walls around her and sitting tight. The card also indicates Marcia's fear of not having enough material security if she leaves the relationship.

Card 5. Nine of Wands

Since this card shows what is moving out of Marcia's life, it seems her need to be on the defensive is losing its importance. The nines symbolize completion and the end of a cycle. Marcia is being asked to make a final step but she has to be strong enough to take the consequences.

Card 6. Four of Wands

The four of wands is a very fortunate card to have in this position. It indicates a period of stability coming into Marcia's life; it seems Marcia will make a decision and it will be the right one for her. The four of wands is about celebration after leaving the old way of life behind.

Card 7. Five of Cups

Even though Marcia might make the right decision, she will also experience heartache and loss. All the fives bring change, and letting go of old patterns always has the price of pain attached. Feelings of loss are always temporary with this card. Marcia needs to grieve in order to move on.

Card 8. Five of Pentacles

Marcia's experience in the relationship has obviously had a very debilitating effect on her, for this card in this position shows she lacks confidence and self-esteem. She may even start to regret the course taken.

Card 9. The Chariot

The Chariot, suggests Marcia needs to take charge of her feelings. She needs to allow her head and not her heart to rule this situation. With the Chariot in the environment, it seems life is telling Marcia to overcome her fears. It is time to gain control over her life and move on.

Card 10. Two of Cups

This is a very positive card in this position; it indicates all Marcia's fears are ungrounded. A relationship is now possible where two people can meet equally, exchanging cups of love and friendship.

Card 11. Four of Cups

There is something being offered to Marcia. She is unaware of the possibilities of the fourth cup, and is perhaps a little afraid to look in case it is more of what she has just experienced. Cards 12 and 13, princess of cups and the Star, indicate the fourth cup offers happiness and love. This is tentative initially, but holds the promise of deep fulfillment and a sense of inner unity.

SUGGESTED READINGS

Arroyo S. Astrology and the Four Elements. CRCS
Nevada, 1975.

Bullfinch Mythology. Random House. New York, 1993.

Campbell, J. *Myths to Live By.* Arkana. New York, 1993.

Campbell, J. *The Hero with a Thousand Faces.* Fontana Press.
London, 1993.

Campbell, J. and Moyers B. *The Power of Myth.* Doubleday.
New York, 1988.

Cirlot, J. E. *A Dictionary of Symbols.* Routledge. London, 1995.

Clarke, B. *Keys to Understanding Chiron.* Astro*Synthesis.
Victoria, Australia, 1992.

Forrest, S. *The InnerSky.* ACS Publications.

Fortune, D. *The Mystical Qabalah.* Aquarian Press. London, 1987.

Frazer, Sir J. *The Golden Bough.* Macmillan. New York, 1947.

Gad, Dr. I. *Tarot and Individuation.* Nicolas-Hays. York Beach,
Maine, 1994.

George, D. *Mysteries of the Dark Moon.* Harper Collins. San
Francisco, 1992.

Graves, R. *The Greek Myths Vols. 1 & 2.* Penguin. UK, 1995.

Graves, R. *The White Goddess.* Faber and Faber. UK, 1948.

Greene, L. Relating: *An Astrological Guide to Living with Others on a Small Planet.* Samuel Weiser. York Beach, Maine, 1984.

Greene, L. *The Astrology of Fate.* Unwin. London, 1985.

Howell, Alice O. *Jungian Symbolism in Astrology.* The Theosophical Publishing House. Wheaton, Illinois, 1987.

Larousse Encyclopedia of Mythology. Hamlyn. England, 1986.

Lyle, J. *Tarot.* Hamlyn Publishing Group. London, 1990.

Matthews, C. *The Celtic Tradition.* Element Books. Dorset, UK, 1989.

Monaghan, P. *The Book of Goddesses and Heroines.* Llewellyn. Minnesota, 1990.

Murray, A.S. *Manual of Mythology.* Tudor Publishing. New York, 1950.

Nichols, S. *Jung and the Tarot; an Archetypal Journey.* Samuel Weiser. York Beach, Maine, 1980.

Ovid Project: http://www.uvm.edu/~hag/ovid.

Rutherford, W. *Celtic Mythology.* Aquarian Press. Northamptonshire, UK, 1987.

The Holy Bible, Revised Standard Edition.

Walker, Barbara G. *The Woman's Encyclopedia of Myths and Secrets.* Harper and Row. New York, 1983.

ENDNOTES

1   Campbell, J. and Moyers, B. *The Power of Myth*, p. 197.

2   Graves, R. *The White Goddess*, p. 157.

3   Walker, Barbara G. *The Woman's Encyclopedia of Myths and Secrets*, p. 951.

4   Graves, R. *The White Goddess*, p. 417

5   *The Holy Bible*, Revised Standard Version. The Wisdom of Solomon, p. 17.

6   Monaghan, P. *The Book of Goddesses and Heroines*, p. 176.

7   Campbell and Moyers, p. 217.

8   Ovid Project: http://www.uvm.edu/~hag/ovid.

9   Cirlot, p. 43.

10 Graves, R. *The Greek Myths Vol. 2*, p. 124b.

11 Monaghan, p. 174.

12 Cirlot, p. 190.

13 Graves. *The White Goddess*, p. 380.

14 Graves. *The White Goddess*, p. 376.

15 Walker, p. 561.

16 Graves. *The Greek Myths Vol. 1*, p. 14.4.

17 *Larousse Encyclopedia of Mythology*, p. 165.

18 Graves. *The White Goddess*, p. 387.

19 *The Holy Bible*. Genesis 3: 22-24.

20 Walker, p. 553.

21 Cirlot, p. 345.

22 Monaghan, p. 178.

23 Murray, A.S. *Manual of Mythology*, p. 186.

[24] Campbell, J. *The Hero with a Thousand Faces*, p. 35.

[25] Campbell, p. 35.

[26] Arroyo, S. *Astrology and the Four Elements*, p. 75.

ABOUT THE AUTHOR

Kay Steventon

When Kay Steventon graduated in 1980 with a diploma of Fine Art from PIT in Melbourne, Australia, she began a serious study of Astrology which led to a Practitioners Certificate from the Federation of Australian Astrologers.

Since then, Kay has had many successful exhibitions of her art and considerable teaching experience. Her parallel work as a professional astrologer led to a deep involvement in the Tarot and the study of mythology. As a result, her art has evolved; she has moved away from the mainstream contemporary work she once favored and now specializes in symbolism.

NOTES

NOTES

NOTES